WORLD ATLAS

Contents

RAND McNALLY & COMPANY

DAVID C. WEST

World Political Information Table

This table gives the area, population, population density, political status, capital, and predominant languages for every country in the world. The political units listed are categorized by political status in the form of government column as follows: A—independent countries; B—internally independent political entities which are under the protection of another country in matters of defense and foreign affairs; C—colonies and other dependent political units; and D—the major administrative subdivisions of Australia, Canada, China, the United Kingdom, and the United States. For comparison, the table also includes the continents and the world. A key to abbreviations of country names appears on page 55. All footnotes to this table appear on page 6.

The populations are estimates for January 1, 1993, made by Rand McNally on the basis of official data, United Nations estimates, and other available information. Area figures include inland water.

REGION OR POLITICAL DIVISION	Area Sq. Mi.	Est. Pop. 1/1/93	Pop. Per. Sq. Mi.	Form of Government and Ruling Power		Capital	Predominant Languages
Afars and Issas see Djibouti							
†Afghanistan	251,826	16,290,000	65	Islamic republic	A	Kābul	Dari, Pashto, Uzbek, Turkmen
Africa	11,700,000	668,700,000	57				
Alabama	52,423	4,128,000	79	State (U.S.)	D	Montgomery	English
Alaska	656,424	564,000	0.9	State (U.S.)	D	Juneau	English, indigenous
†Albania	11,100	3,305,000	298	Republic	A	Tiranë	Albanian, Greek
Alberta	255,287	2,839,000	11	Province (Canada)	D	Edmonton	English
†Algeria	919,595	26,925,000	29	Provisional military government	A	Algiers (El Djazaïr)	Arabic, Berber dialects, French
American Samoa	77	52,000	675	Unincorporated territory (U.S.)	C	Pago Pago	Samoan, English
†Andorra	175	56,000	320	Coprincipality (Spanish and French protection)	B	Andorra	Catalan, Castilian, French
†Angola	481,354	10,735,000	22	Republic	A	Luanda	Portuguese, indigenous
Anguilla	35	7,000	200	Dependent territory (U.K. protection)	B	The Valley	English
Anhui	53,668	58,440,000	1,089	Province (China)	D	Hefei	Chinese (Mandarin)
Antarctica	5,400,000	(1)					
†Antigua and Barbuda	171	77,000	450	Parliamentary state	A	St. John's	English, local dialects
†Argentina	1,073,519	32,950,000	31	Republic	A	Buenos Aires and Viedma (6)	Spanish, English, Italian, German, French
Arizona	114,006	3,872,000	34	State (U.S.)	D	Phoenix	English
Arkansas	53,182	2,410,000	45	State (U.S.)	D	Little Rock	English
†Armenia	11,506	3,429,000	298	Republic	A	Yerevan	Armenian, Russian
Aruba	75	65,000	867	Self-governing territory (Netherlands protection)	B	Oranjestad	Dutch, Papiamento, English, Spanish
Ascension	34	1,200	35	Dependency (St. Helena)	C	Georgetown	English
Asia	17,300,000	3,337,800,000	193				
†Australia	2,966,155	16,965,000	5.7	Federal parliamentary state	A	Canberra	English, indigenous
Australian Capital Territory	927	282,000	304	Territory (Australia)	D	Canberra	English
†Austria	32,377	7,899,000	244	Federal republic	A	Vienna (Wien)	German
†Azerbaijan	33,436	7,510,000	225	Republic	A	Baku (Bakı)	Azeri, Russian, Armenian
†Bahamas	5,382	265,000	49	Parliamentary state	A	Nassau	English, Creole
†Bahrain	267	561,000	2,101	Monarchy	A	Al Manāmah	Arabic, English, Farsi, Urdu
†Bangladesh	55,598	120,850,000	2,174	Republic	A	Dhaka	Bangla, English
†Barbados	166	258,000	1,554	Parliamentary state	A	Bridgetown	English
Beijing (Peking)	6,487	11,290,000	1,740	Autonomous city (China)	D	Beijing (Peking)	Chinese (Mandarin)
†Belarus	80,155	10,400,000	130	Republic	A	Minsk	Byelorussian, Russian
Belau see Palau							
†Belgium	11,783	10,030,000	851	Constitutional monarchy	A	Brussels (Bruxelles)	Dutch (Flemish), French, German
†Belize	8,866	186,000	21	Parliamentary state	A	Belmopan	English, Spanish, Mayan, Garifuna
†Benin	43,475	5,083,000	117	Republic	A	Porto-Novo and Cotonou	French, Fon, Adja, Yoruba, indigenous
Bermuda	21	60,000	2,857	Dependent territory (U.K.)	C	Hamilton	English
†Bhutan	17,954	1,680,000	94	Monarchy (Indian protection)	B	Thimphu	Dzongkha, Tibetan and Nepalese dialects
†Bolivia	424,165	7,411,000	17	Republic	A	La Paz and Sucre	Aymara, Quechua, Spanish
Bophuthatswana (2)	15,641	2,525,000	161	National state (South African protection)	B	Mmabatho	Tswana
†Bosnia and Herzegovina	19,741	4,375,000	222	Republic	A	Sarajevo	Serbian, Croatian
†Botswana	224,711	1,379,000	6.1	Republic	A	Gaborone	English, Tswana
†Brazil	3,286,500	159,630,000	49	Federal republic	A	Brasília	Portuguese, Spanish, English, French
British Columbia	365,948	3,665,000	10	Province (Canada)	D	Victoria	English
British Indian Ocean Territory	23	(1)		Dependent territory (U.K.)	C		English
†Brunei	2,226	273,000	123	Monarchy	A	Bandar Seri Begawan	Malay, English, Chinese
†Bulgaria	42,823	8,842,000	206	Republic	A	Sofia (Sofiya)	Bulgarian
†Burkina Faso	105,869	9,808,000	93	Provisional military government	A	Ouagadougou	French, indigenous
Burma see Myanmar							
†Burundi	10,745	6,118,000	569	Republic	A	Bujumbura	French, Kirundi, Swahili
California	163,707	31,310,000	191	State (U.S.)	D	Sacramento	English
†Cambodia	69,898	8,928,000	128	Transitional government	A	Phnum Pénh (Phnom Penh)	Khmer, French
†Cameroon	183,569	12,875,000	70	Republic	A	Yaoundé	English, French, indigenous
†Canada	3,849,674	30,530,000	7.9	Federal parliamentary state	A	Ottawa	English, French
†Cape Verde	1,557	404,000	259	Republic	A	Praia	Portuguese, Crioulo
Cayman Islands	100	29,000	290	Dependent territory (U.K.)	C	Georgetown	English
†Central African Republic	240,535	3,068,000	13	Republic	A	Bangui	French, Sango, Arabic, indigenous
Ceylon see Sri Lanka							
†Chad	495,755	5,297,000	11	Republic	A	N'Djamena	Arabic, French, indigenous
Channel Islands	75	143,000	1,907	Dependent territory (U.K.)	B		English, French
†Chile	292,135	13,635,000	47	Republic	A	Santiago	Spanish
†China (excl. Taiwan)	3,689,631	1,179,030,000	320	Socialist republic	A	Beijing (Peking)	Chinese dialects
Christmas Island	52	900	17	External territory (Australia)	C	The Settlement	English, Chinese, Malay
Ciskei (2)	2,996	1,105,000	369	National state (South African protection)	B	Bisho	English, Xhosa, Afrikaans
Cocos (Keeling) Islands	5.4	500	93	Territory (Australia)	C		English, Cocos-Malay, Malay
†Colombia	440,831	34,640,000	79	Republic	A	Santa Fe de Bogotá	Spanish
Colorado	104,100	3,410,000	33	State (U.S.)	D	Denver	English
†Comoros (excl. Mayotte)	863	503,000	583	Federal Islamic republic	A	Moroni	Arabic, French, Comoran
†Congo	132,047	2,413,000	18	Republic	A	Brazzaville	French, Lingala, Kikongo, indigenous
Connecticut	5,544	3,358,000	606	State (U.S.)	D	Hartford	English
Cook Islands	91	18,000	198	Self-governing territory (New Zealand protection)	B	Avarua	English, Maori
†Costa Rica	19,730	3,225,000	163	Republic	A	San José	Spanish

REGION OR POLITICAL DIVISION	Area Sq. Mi.	Est. Pop. 1/1/93	Pop. Per. Sq. Mi.	Form of Government and Ruling Power		Capital	Predominant Languages
† Cote d'Ivoire	124,518	13,765,000	111	Republic	A	Abidjan and Yamoussoukro (6)	French, indigenous
† Croatia	21,829	4,793,000	220	Republic	A	Zagreb	Croatian, Serbian
† Cuba	42,804	10,900,000	255	Socialist republic	A	Havana (La Habana)	Spanish
† Cyprus	2,276	527,000	232	Republic	A	Nicosia (Levkosía)	Greek, English
Cyprus, North (3)	1,295	193,000	149	Republic	A	Nicosia (Lefkoşa)	Turkish
† Czech Republic	30,450	10,335,000	339	Republic	A	Prague (Praha)	Czech, Slovak
Delaware	2,489	692,000	278	State (U.S.)	D	Dover	English
† Denmark	16,638	5,169,000	311	Constitutional monarchy	A	Copenhagen (København)	Danish
District of Columbia	68	590,000	8,676	Federal district (U.S.)	D	Washington	English
† Djibouti	8,958	396,000	44	Republic	A	Djibouti	French, Arabic, Somali, Afar
† Dominica	305	88,000	289	Republic	A	Roseau	English, French
† Dominican Republic	18,704	7,591,000	406	Republic	A	Santo Domingo	Spanish
† Ecuador	109,484	11,055,000	101	Republic	A	Quito	Spanish, Quechua, indigenous
† Egypt	386,662	57,050,000	148	Socialist republic	A	Cairo (Al Qāhirah)	Arabic
Ellice Islands see Tuvalu							
† El Salvador	8,124	5,635,000	694	Republic	A	San Salvador	Spanish, Nahua
England	50,378	48,235,000	957	Administrative division (U.K.)	D	London	English
† Equatorial Guinea	10,831	394,000	36	Republic	A	Malabo	Spanish, indigenous, English
† Eritrea	36,170	3,425,000	95	Republic	A	Asmera	Tigrinya, Tigre, Arabic, Saho, Agau
† Estonia	17,413	1,613,000	93	Republic	A	Tallinn	Estonian, Russian
† Ethiopia	446,953	51,715,000	116	Transitional military government	A	Addis Ababa	Amharic, Tigrinya, Orominga, Guaraginga, Somali, Arabic
Europe	3,800,000	694,900,000	183				
Faeroe Islands	540	49,000	91	Self-governing territory (Danish protection)	B	Tórshavn	Danish, Faroese
Falkland Islands (4)	4,700	2,100	0.4	Dependent territory (U.K.)	C	Stanley	English
† Fiji	7,056	754,000	107	Republic	A	Suva	English, Fijian, Hindustani
† Finland	130,559	5,074,000	39	Republic	A	Helsinki (Helsingfors)	Finnish, Swedish
Florida	65,758	13,630,000	207	State (U.S.)	D	Tallahassee	English
† France (excl. Overseas Departments)	211,208	57,570,000	273	Republic	A	Paris	French
French Guiana	35,135	131,000	3.7	Overseas department (France)	C	Cayenne	French
French Polynesia	1,359	208,000	153	Overseas territory (France)	C	Papeete	French, Tahitian
Fujian	46,332	31,160,000	673	Province (China)	D	Fuzhou	Chinese dialects
† Gabon	103,347	1,115,000	11	Republic	A	Libreville	French, Fang, indigenous
† Gambia	4,127	916,000	222	Republic	A	Banjul	English, Malinke, Wolof, Fula, indigenous
Gansu	173,746	23,280,000	134	Province (China)	D	Lanzhou	Chinese (Mandarin), Mongolian, Tibetan dialects
Georgia	59,441	6,795,000	114	State (U.S.)	D	Atlanta	English
† Georgia	26,911	5,593,000	208	Provisional military government	A	Tbilisi	Georgian, Russian, Armenian, Azerbaijani
† Germany	137,822	80,590,000	585	Federal republic	A	Berlin and Bonn	German
† Ghana	92,098	16,445,000	179	Provisional military government	A	Accra	English, Akanand other indigenous
Gibraltar	2.3	32,000	13,913	Dependent territory (U.K.)	C	Gibraltar	English, Spanish
Gilbert Islands see Kiribati							
Great Britain see United Kingdom							
† Greece	50,949	10,075,000	198	Republic	A	Athens (Athínai)	Greek
Greenland	840,004	57,000	0.1	Self-governing territory (Danish protection)	B	Godthåb	Danish, Greenlandic, Inuit dialects
† Grenada	133	97,000	729	Parliamentary state	A	St. George's	English, French
Guadeloupe (incl. Dependencies)	687	413,000	601	Overseas department (France)	C	Basse-Terre	French, Creole
Guam	209	143,000	684	Unincorporated territory (U.S.)	C	Agana	English, Chamorro
Guangdong	68,726	65,380,000	951	Province (China)	D	Guangzhou (Canton)	Chinese dialects, Miao-Yao
Guangxi Zhuangzu	91,236	43,975,000	482	Autonomous region (China)	D	Nanning	Chinese dialects, Thai, Miao-Yao
† Guatemala	42,042	9,705,000	231	Republic	A	Guatemala	Spanish, indigenous
Guernsey (incl. Dependencies)	30	58,000	1,933	Crown dependency (U.K. protection)	B	St. Peter Port	English, French
† Guinea	94,926	7,726,000	81	Provisional military government	A	Conakry	French, indigenous
† Guinea-Bissau	13,948	1,060,000	76	Republic	A	Bissau	Portuguese, Crioulo, indigenous
Guizhou	65,637	33,745,000	514	Province (China)	D	Guiyang	Chinese (Mandarin), Thai, Miao-Yao
† Guyana	83,000	737,000	8.9	Republic	A	Georgetown	English, indigenous
Hainan	13,127	6,820,000	520	Province (China)	D	Haikou	Chinese, Min, Tai
† Haiti	10,714	6,509,000	608	Provisional military government	A	Port-au-Prince	Creole, French
Hawaii	10,932	1,159,000	106	State (U.S.)	D	Honolulu	English, Hawaiian, Japanese
Hebei	73,359	63,500,000	866	Province (China)	D	Shijiazhuang	Chinese (Mandarin)
Heilongjiang	181,082	36,685,000	203	Province (China)	D	Harbin	Chinese dialects, Mongolian, Tungus
Henan	64,479	88,890,000	1,379	Province (China)	D	Zhengzhou	Chinese (Mandarin)
Holland see Netherlands							
† Honduras	43,277	5,164,000	119	Republic	A	Tegucigalpa	Spanish, indigenous
Hong Kong	414	5,580,000	13,478	Chinese territory under British administration	C	Victoria (Hong Kong)	Chinese (Cantonese), English, Putonghua
Hubei	72,356	56,090,000	775	Province (China)	D	Wuhan	Chinese dialects
Hunan	81,081	63,140,000	779	Province (China)	D	Changsha	Chinese dialects, Miao-Yao
† Hungary	35,920	10,305,000	287	Republic	A	Budapest	Hungarian
† Iceland	39,769	260,000	6.5	Republic	A	Reykjavík	Icelandic
Idaho	83,574	1,026,000	12	State (U.S.)	D	Boise	English
Illinois	57,918	11,640,000	201	State (U.S.)	D	Springfield	English
† India (incl. part of Jammu and Kashmir)	1,237,062	873,850,000	706	Federal republic	A	New Delhi	English, Hindi, Telugu, Bengali, indigenous
Indiana	36,420	5,667,000	156	State (U.S.)	D	Indianapolis	English
† Indonesia	752,410	186,180,000	247	Republic	A	Jakarta	Bahasa Indonesia (Malay), English, Dutch, indigenous
Iowa	56,276	2,821,000	50	State (U.S.)	D	Des Moines	English
† Iran	632,457	60,500,000	96	Islamic republic	A	Tehrān	Farsi, Turkish dialects
† Iraq	169,235	18,815,000	111	Republic	A	Baghdād	Arabic, Kurdish, Assyrian, Armenian
† Ireland	27,137	3,525,000	130	Republic	A	Dublin (Baile Átha Cliath)	English, Irish Gaelic
Isle of Man	221	70,000	317	Crown dependency (U.K. protection)	B	Douglas	English, Manx Gaelic
† Israel (excl. Occupied Areas)	8,019	4,593,000	573	Republic	A	Jerusalem (Yerushalayim)	Hebrew, Arabic
Israeli Occupied Areas (5)	2,947	2,461,000	835	None			Arabic, Hebrew, English
† Italy	116,324	56,550,000	486	Republic	A	Rome (Roma)	Italian
Ivory Coast see Cote d'Ivoire							

REGION OR POLITICAL DIVISION	Area Sq. Mi.	Est. Pop. 1/1/93	Pop. Per. Sq. Mi.	Form of Government and Ruling Power	Capital	Predominant Languages
† Jamaica	4,244	2,412,000	568	Parliamentary state .... A	Kingston	English, Creole
† Japan	145,870	124,710,000	855	Constitutional monarchy .... A	Tōkyō	Japanese
Jersey	45	85,000	1,889	Crown dependency (U.K. protection) .... B	St. Helier	English, French
Jiangsu	39,614	69,730,000	1,760	Province (China) .... D	Nanjing (Nanking)	Chinese dialects
Jiangxi	64,325	39,270,000	610	Province (China) .... D	Nanchang	Chinese dialects
Jilin	72,201	25,630,000	355	Province (China) .... D	Changchun	Chinese (Mandarin), Mongolian, Korean
† Jordan (excl. West Bank)	35,135	3,632,000	103	Constitutional monarchy .... A	'Ammān	Arabic
Kansas	82,282	2,539,000	31	State (U.S.) .... D	Topeka	English
† Kazakhstan	1,049,156	17,190,000	16	Republic .... A	Alma-Ata (Almaty)	Kazakh, Russian
Kentucky	40,411	3,745,000	93	State (U.S.) .... D	Frankfort	English
† Kenya	224,961	26,635,000	118	Republic .... A	Nairobi	English, Swahili, indigenous
Kiribati	313	76,000	243	Republic .... A	Bairiki	English, Gilbertese
† Korea, North	46,540	22,450,000	482	Socialist republic .... A	Pyŏngyang	Korean
† Korea, South	38,230	43,660,000	1,142	Republic .... A	Seoul (Sŏul)	Korean
† Kuwait	6,880	2,388,000	347	Constitutional monarchy .... A	Kuwait	Arabic, English
† Kyrgyzstan	76,641	4,613,000	60	Republic .... A	Bishkek	Kirghiz, Russian, Uzbek
† Laos	91,429	4,507,000	49	Socialist republic .... A	Viangchan (Vientiane)	Lao, French, indigenous
† Latvia	24,595	2,737,000	111	Republic .... A	Rīga	Latvian, Russian, Lithuanian
† Lebanon	4,015	3,467,000	864	Republic .... A	Beirut (Bayrūt)	Arabic, French, Armenian, English
† Lesotho	11,720	1,873,000	160	Constitutional monarchy under military rule A	Maseru	English, Sesotho, Zulu, Xhosa
Liaoning	56,255	41,035,000	729	Province (China) .... D	Shenyang	Chinese (Mandarin), Mongolian
† Liberia	38,250	2,869,000	75	Republic .... A	Monrovia	English, indigenous
† Libya	679,362	4,552,000	6.7	Socialist republic .... A	Tripoli (Ṭarābulus)	Arabic
† Liechtenstein	62	30,000	484	Constitutional monarchy .... A	Vaduz	German
† Lithuania	25,174	3,804,000	151	Republic .... A	Vilnius	Lithuanian, Russian, Polish
Louisiana	51,843	4,282,000	83	State (U.S.) .... D	Baton Rouge	English
† Luxembourg	998	392,000	393	Constitutional monarchy .... A	Luxembourg	French, Luxembourgish, German
Macao	6.6	477,000	72,273	Chinese territory under Portuguese administration C	Macao	Portuguese, Chinese (Cantonese)
† Macedonia	9,928	2,179,000	219	Republic .... A	Skopje	Macedonian, Albanian
† Madagascar	226,658	12,800,000	56	Republic .... A	Antananarivo	Malagasy, French
Maine	35,387	1,257,000	36	State (U.S.) .... D	Augusta	English
† Malawi	45,747	9,691,000	212	Republic .... A	Lilongwe	Chichewa, English
† Malaysia	129,251	18,630,000	144	Federal constitutional monarchy ... A	Kuala Lumpur	Malay, Chinese dialects, English, Tamil
† Maldives	115	235,000	2,043	Republic .... A	Male	Divehi
† Mali	482,077	8,754,000	18	Republic .... A	Bamako	French, Bambara, indigenous
† Malta	122	360,000	2,951	Republic .... A	Valletta	English, Maltese
Manitoba	250,947	1,221,000	4.9	Province (Canada) .... D	Winnipeg	English
† Marshall Islands	70	51,000	729	Republic (U.S. protection) .... A	Majuro (island)	English, indigenous, Japanese
Martinique	425	372,000	875	Overseas department (France) C	Fort-de-France	French, Creole
Maryland	12,407	4,975,000	401	State (U.S.) .... D	Annapolis	English
Massachusetts	10,555	6,103,000	578	State (U.S.) .... D	Boston	English
† Mauritania	395,956	2,092,000	5.3	Republic .... A	Nouakchott	Arabic, Pular, Soninke, Wolof
† Mauritius (incl. Dependencies)	788	1,096,000	1,391	Republic .... A	Port Louis	English, Creole, Bhojpuri, French, Hindi, Tamil, others
Mayotte [7]	144	89,000	618	Territorial collectivity (France) C	Dzaoudzi and Mamoudzou [6]	French, Swahili (Mahorian)
† Mexico	759,534	86,170,000	113	Federal republic .... A	Mexico City (Ciudad de México)	Spanish, indigenous
Michigan	96,810	9,488,000	98	State (U.S.) .... D	Lansing	English
† Micronesia, Federated States of	271	117,000	432	Republic (U.S. protection) .... A	Kolonia and Paliker [6]	English, indigenous
Midway Islands	2.0	500	250	Unincorporated territory (U.S.) C	....	English
Minnesota	86,943	4,513,000	52	State (U.S.) .... D	St. Paul	English
Mississippi	48,434	2,616,000	54	State (U.S.) .... D	Jackson	English
Missouri	69,709	5,231,000	75	State (U.S.) .... D	Jefferson City	English
† Moldova	13,012	4,474,000	344	Republic .... A	Kishinev (Chişinău)	Romanian (Moldovan), Russian
† Monaco	0.7	31,000	44,286	Constitutional monarchy .... A	Monaco	French, English, Italian, Monegasque
† Mongolia	604,829	2,336,000	3.9	Republic .... A	Ulan Bator (Ulaanbaatar)	Khalkha Mongol, Turkish dialects, Russian, Chinese
Montana	147,046	821,000	5.6	State (U.S.) .... D	Helena	English
Montserrat	39	13,000	333	Dependent territory (U.K.) C	Plymouth	English
† Morocco (excl. Western Sahara)	172,414	27,005,000	157	Constitutional monarchy .... A	Rabat	Arabic, Berber dialects, French
† Mozambique	308,642	15,795,000	51	Republic .... A	Maputo	Portuguese, indigenous
† Myanmar	261,228	43,070,000	165	Provisional military government .... A	Rangoon (Yangon)	Burmese, indigenous
† Namibia (excl. Walvis Bay)	317,818	1,603,000	5.0	Republic .... A	Windhoek	English, Afrikaans, German, indigenous
Nauru	8.1	10,000	1,235	Republic .... A	Yaren District	Nauruan, English
Nebraska	77,358	1,615,000	21	State (U.S.) .... D	Lincoln	English
Nei Monggol (Inner Mongolia)	456,759	22,340,000	49	Autonomous region (China) .... D	Hohhot	Mongolian
† Nepal	56,827	20,325,000	358	Constitutional monarchy .... A	Kathmandu	Nepali, Maithali, Bhojpuri, other indigenous
† Netherlands	16,164	15,190,000	940	Constitutional monarchy .... A	Amsterdam and The Hague ('s-Gravenhage)	Dutch
Netherlands Antilles	309	191,000	618	Self-governing territory (Netherlands protection) .... B	Willemstad	Dutch, Papiamento, English
Nevada	110,567	1,308,000	12	State (U.S.) .... D	Carson City	English
New Brunswick	28,355	824,000	29	Province (Canada) .... D	Fredericton	English, French
New Caledonia	7,358	177,000	24	Overseas territory (France) C	Nouméa	French, indigenous
Newfoundland	156,649	641,000	4.1	Province (Canada) .... D	St. John's	English
New Hampshire	9,351	1,154,000	123	State (U.S.) .... D	Concord	English
New Hebrides see Vanuatu						
New Jersey	8,722	7,898,000	906	State (U.S.) .... D	Trenton	English
New Mexico	121,598	1,590,000	13	State (U.S.) .... D	Santa Fe	English, Spanish
New South Wales	309,500	5,770,000	19	State (Australia) .... D	Sydney	English
New York	54,475	18,350,000	337	State (U.S.) .... D	Albany	English
† New Zealand	104,454	3,477,000	33	Parliamentary state .... A	Wellington	English, Maori
† Nicaragua	50,054	3,932,000	79	Republic .... A	Managua	Spanish, English, indigenous
† Niger	489,191	8,198,000	17	Provisional military government .... A	Niamey	French, Hausa, Djerma, indigenous
† Nigeria	356,669	91,700,000	257	Provisional military government .... A	Lagos and Abuja	English, Hausa, Fulani, Yoruba, Ibo, indigenous
Ningxia Huizu	25,637	4,820,000	188	Autonomous region (China) .... D	Yinchuan	Chinese (Mandarin)

REGION OR POLITICAL DIVISION	Area Sq. Mi.	Est. Pop. 1/1/93	Pop. Per. Sq. Mi.	Form of Government and Ruling Power		Capital	Predominant Languages
Niue	100	1,700	17	Self-governing territory (New Zealand protection)	B	Alofi	English, indigenous
Norfolk Island	14	2,600	186	External territory (Australia)	C	Kingston	English, Norfolk
North America	9,500,000	438,200,000	46				
North Carolina	53,821	6,846,000	127	State (U.S.)	D	Raleigh	English
North Dakota	70,704	632,000	8.9	State (U.S.)	D	Bismarck	English
Northern Ireland	5,452	1,604,000	294	Administrative division (U.K.)	D	Belfast	English
Northern Mariana Islands	184	48,000	261	Commonwealth (U.S. protection)	B	Saipan (island)	English, Chamorro, Carolinian
Northern Territory	519,771	176,000	0.3	Territory (Australia)	D	Darwin	English, indigenous
Northwest Territories	1,322,910	61,000	....	Territory (Canada)	D	Yellowknife	English, indigenous
† Norway (incl. Svalbard and Jan Mayen)	149,412	4,308,000	29	Constitutional monarchy	A	Oslo	Norwegian, Lapp, Finnish
Nova Scotia	21,425	1,007,000	47	Province (Canada)	D	Halifax	English
Oceania (incl. Australia)	3,300,000	26,700,000	8.1				
Ohio	44,828	11,025,000	246	State (U.S.)	D	Columbus	English
Oklahoma	69,903	3,205,000	46	State (U.S.)	D	Oklahoma City	English
† Oman	82,030	1,617,000	20	Monarchy	A	Muscat	Arabic, English, Baluchi, Urdu, Indian dialects
Ontario	412,581	11,265,000	27	Province (Canada)	D	Toronto	English
Oregon	98,386	2,949,000	30	State (U.S.)	D	Salem	English
† Pakistan (incl. part of Jammu and Kashmir)	339,732	123,490,000	363	Federal Islamic republic	A	Islāmābād	English, Urdu, Punjabi, Sindhi, Pashto
Palau (Belau)	196	16,000	82	Under U.S. administration	B	Koror and Melekeok (6)	English, Palauan, Sonsololese, Tobi
† Panama	29,157	2,555,000	88	Republic	A	Panamá	Spanish, English
† Papua New Guinea	178,704	3,737,000	21	Parliamentary state	A	Port Moresby	English, Motu, Pidgin, indigenous
† Paraguay	157,048	5,003,000	32	Republic	A	Asunción	Spanish, Guarani
Pennsylvania	46,058	12,105,000	263	State (U.S.)	D	Harrisburg	English
† Peru	496,225	22,995,000	46	Republic	A	Lima	Quechua, Spanish, Aymara
† Philippines	115,831	65,500,000	565	Republic	A	Manila	English, Pilipino, Tagalog
Pitcairn (incl. Dependencies)	19	50	2.6	Dependent territory (U.K.)	C	Adamstown	English, Tahitian
† Poland	120,728	38,330,000	317	Republic	A	Warsaw (Warszawa)	Polish
† Portugal	35,516	10,660,000	300	Republic	A	Lisbon (Lisboa)	Portuguese
Prince Edward Island	2,185	152,000	70	Province (Canada)	D	Charlottetown	English
Puerto Rico	3,515	3,594,000	1,022	Commonwealth (U.S. protection)	B	San Juan	Spanish, English
† Qatar	4,412	492,000	112	Monarchy	A	Doha	Arabic, English
Qinghai	277,994	4,585,000	16	Province (China)	D	Xining	Tibetan dialects, Mongolian, Turkish dialects, Chinese (Mandarin)
Quebec	594,860	7,725,000	13	Province (Canada)	D	Québec	French, English
Queensland	666,876	3,000,000	4.5	State (Australia)	D	Brisbane	English
Reunion	969	633,000	653	Overseas department (France)	C	Saint-Denis	French, Creole
Rhode Island	1,545	1,026,000	664	State (U.S.)	D	Providence	English
Rhodesia see Zimbabwe							
† Romania	91,699	23,200,000	253	Republic	A	Bucharest (Bucureşti)	Romanian, Hungarian, German
† Russia	6,592,849	150,500,000	23	Republic	A	Moscow (Moskva)	Russian, Tatar, Ukrainian
† Rwanda	10,169	7,573,000	745	Provisional military government	A	Kigali	French, Kinyarwanda
St. Helena (incl. Dependencies)	121	7,000	58	Dependent territory (U.K.)	C	Jamestown	English
† St. Kitts and Nevis	104	40,000	385	Parliamentary state	A	Basseterre	English
† St. Lucia	238	153,000	643	Parliamentary state	A	Castries	English, French
St. Pierre and Miquelon	93	7,000	75	Territorial collectivity (France)	C	Saint-Pierre	French
† St. Vincent and the Grenadines	150	116,000	773	Parliamentary state	A	Kingstown	English, French
† San Marino	24	23,000	958	Republic	A	San Marino	Italian
† Sao Tome and Principe	372	134,000	360	Republic	A	São Tomé	Portuguese, Fang
Saskatchewan	251,866	1,099,000	4.4	Province (Canada)	D	Regina	English
† Saudi Arabia	830,000	15,985,000	19	Monarchy	A	Riyadh (Ar Riyāḍ)	Arabic
Scotland	30,421	5,145,000	169	Administrative division (U.K.)	D	Edinburgh	English, Scots Gaelic
† Senegal	75,951	7,849,000	103	Republic	A	Dakar	French, Wolof, Fulani, Serer, indigenous
† Seychelles	175	70,000	400	Republic	A	Victoria	English, French, Creole
Shaanxi	79,151	34,215,000	432	Province (China)	D	Xi'an (Sian)	Chinese (Mandarin)
Shandong	59,074	87,840,000	1,487	Province (China)	D	Jinan	Chinese (Mandarin)
Shanghai	2,394	13,875,000	5,796	Autonomous city (China)	D	Shanghai	Chinese (Wu)
Shanxi	60,232	29,865,000	496	Province (China)	D	Taiyuan	Chinese (Mandarin)
Sichuan	220,078	111,470,000	507	Province (China)	D	Chengdu	Chinese (Mandarin), Tibetan dialects, Miao-Yao
† Sierra Leone	27,925	4,424,000	158	Transitional military government	A	Freetown	English, Krio, indigenous
† Singapore	246	2,812,000	11,431	Republic	A	Singapore	Chinese (Mandarin), English, Malay, Tamil
† Slovakia	18,933	5,287,000	279	Republic	A	Bratislava	Slovak, Hungarian
† Slovenia	7,819	1,965,000	251	Republic	A	Ljubljana	Slovenian, Serbian, Croatian
† Solomon Islands	10,954	366,000	33	Parliamentary state	A	Honiara	English, indigenous
† Somalia	246,201	6,000,000	24	None	A	Mogadishu (Muqdisho)	Arabic, Somali, English, Italian
† South Africa (incl. Walvis Bay)	433,680	33,040,000	76	Republic	A	Pretoria, Cape Town, and Bloemfontein	Afrikaans, English, Xhosa, Zulu, other indigenous
South America	6,900,000	310,700,000	45				
South Australia	379,925	1,410,000	3.7	State (Australia)	D	Adelaide	English
South Carolina	32,007	3,616,000	113	State (U.S.)	D	Columbia	English
South Dakota	77,121	718,000	9.3	State (U.S.)	D	Pierre	English
South Georgia (incl. Dependencies)	1,450	(1)	....	Dependent territory (U.K.)	C	Grytviken Harbour	English
South West Africa see Namibia							
† Spain	194,885	39,155,000	201	Constitutional monarchy	A	Madrid	Spanish (Castilian), Catalan, Galician, Basque
Spanish North Africa (8)	12	144,000	12,000	Five possessions (Spain)	C	....	Spanish, Arabic, Berber dialects
Spanish Sahara see Western Sahara							
† Sri Lanka	24,962	17,740,000	711	Socialist republic	A	Colombo and Sri Jayawardenapura	English, Sinhala, Tamil
† Sudan	967,500	28,760,000	30	Provisional military government	A	Khartoum (Al Kharṭūm)	Arabic, Nubian and other indigenous, English
† Suriname	63,251	413,000	6.5	Republic	A	Paramaribo	Dutch, Sranan Tongo, English, Hindustani, Javanese

REGION OR POLITICAL DIVISION	Area Sq. Mi.	Est. Pop. 1/1/93	Pop. Per. Sq. Mi.	Form of Government and Ruling Power	Capital	Predominant Languages
† Swaziland	6,704	925,000	138	Monarchy ... A	Mbabane and Lobamba	English, siSwati
† Sweden	173,732	8,619,000	50	Constitutional monarchy ... A	Stockholm	Swedish, Lapp, Finnish
Switzerland	15,943	6,848,000	430	Federal republic ... A	Bern (Berne)	German, French, Italian, Romansch
† Syria	71,498	14,070,000	197	Socialist republic ... A	Damascus (Dimashq)	Arabic, Kurdish, Armenian, Aramaic, Circassian
Taiwan	13,900	20,985,000	1,510	Republic ... A	T'aipei	Chinese (Mandarin), Miu, Hakka
† Tajikistan	55,251	5,765,000	104	Republic ... A	Dushanbe	Tajik, Uzbek, Russian
† Tanzania	364,900	28,265,000	77	Republic ... A	Dar es Salaam and Dodoma [6]	English, Swahili, indigenous
Tasmania	26,178	456,000	17	State (Australia) ... D	Hobart	English
Tennessee	42,146	5,026,000	119	State (U.S.) ... D	Nashville	English
Texas	268,601	17,610,000	66	State (U.S.) ... D	Austin	English, Spanish
† Thailand	198,115	58,030,000	293	Constitutional monarchy ... A	Bangkok (Krung Thep)	Thai, indigenous
Tianjin (Tientsin)	4,363	9,170,000	2,102	Autonomous city (China) ... D	Tianjin (Tientsin)	Chinese (Mandarin)
† Togo	21,925	4,030,000	184	Provisional military government ... A	Lomé	French, indigenous
Tokelau	4.6	1,800	391	Island territory (New Zealand) ... C	...	English, Tokelauan
Tonga	288	103,000	358	Constitutional monarchy ... A	Nuku'alofa	Tongan, English
Transkei [2]	16,816	4,845,000	288	National state (South African protection) ... B	Umtata	Xhosa, Afrikaans
† Trinidad and Tobago	1,980	1,307,000	660	Republic ... A	Port of Spain	English, Hindi, French, Spanish
Tristan da Cunha	40	300	7.5	Dependency (St. Helena) ... C	Edinburgh	English
† Tunisia	63,170	8,495,000	134	Republic ... A	Tunis	Arabic, French
† Turkey	300,948	58,620,000	195	Republic ... A	Ankara	Turkish, Kurdish, Arabic
† Turkmenistan	188,456	3,884,000	21	Republic ... A	Ashkhabad	Turkmen, Russian, Uzbek, Kazakh
Turks and Caicos Islands	193	13,000	67	Dependent territory (U.K.) ... C	Grand Turk	English
Tuvalu	10	10,000	1,000	Parliamentary state ... A	Funafuti	Tuvaluan, English
† Uganda	93,104	17,410,000	187	Republic ... A	Kampala	English, Luganda, Swahili, indigenous
† Ukraine	233,090	51,990,000	223	Republic ... A	Kiev (Kyyiv)	Ukrainian, Russian, Romanian, Polish
† United Arab Emirates	32,278	2,590,000	80	Federation of monarchs ... A	Abū Ẓaby (Abu Dhabi)	Arabic, English, Farsi, Hindi, Urdu
† United Kingdom	94,269	57,890,000	614	Constitutional monarchy ... A	London	English, Welsh, Gaelic
† United States	3,787,425	256,420,000	68	Federal republic ... A	Washington	English, Spanish
Upper Volta see Burkina Faso	...	...	...	...	...	...
† Uruguay	68,500	3,151,000	46	Republic ... A	Montevideo	Spanish
Utah	84,904	1,795,000	21	State (U.S.) ... D	Salt Lake City	English
† Uzbekistan	172,742	21,885,000	127	Republic ... A	Tashkent	Uzbek, Russian, Kazakh, Tajik, Tatar
† Vanuatu	4,707	157,000	33	Republic ... A	Port Vila	Bislama, English, French
Vatican City	0.2	800	4,000	Monarchical-sacerdotal state ... A	Vatican City	Italian, Latin, other
Venda [2]	2,393	732,000	306	National state (South African protection) ... B	Thohoyandou	Afrikaans, English, Venda
† Venezuela	352,145	19,085,000	54	Federal republic ... A	Caracas	Spanish, indigenous
Vermont	9,615	590,000	61	State (U.S.) ... D	Montpelier	English
Victoria	87,877	4,273,000	49	State (Australia) ... D	Melbourne	English
† Vietnam	127,428	69,650,000	547	Socialist republic ... A	Hanoi	Vietnamese, French, Chinese, English, Khmer, indigenous
Virginia	42,769	6,411,000	150	State (U.S.) ... D	Richmond	English
Virgin Islands (U.S.)	133	104,000	782	Unincorporated territory (U.S.) ... C	Charlotte Amalie	English, Spanish, Creole
Virgin Islands, British	59	13,000	220	Dependent territory (U.K.) ... C	Road Town	English
Wake Island	3.0	200	67	Unincorporated territory (U.S.) ... C	...	English
Wales	8,018	2,906,000	362	Administrative division (U.K.) ... D	Cardiff	English, Welsh Gaelic
Wallis and Futuna	98	17,000	173	Overseas territory (France) ... C	Mata-Utu	French, Uvean, Futunan
Washington	71,303	5,052,000	71	State (U.S.) ... D	Olympia	English
Western Australia	975,101	1,598,000	1.6	State (Australia) ... D	Perth	English
Western Sahara	102,703	200,000	1.9	Occupied by Morocco ... C	...	Arabic
† Western Samoa	1,093	197,000	180	Constitutional monarchy ... A	Apia	English, Samoan
West Virginia	24,231	1,795,000	74	State (U.S.) ... D	Charleston	English
Wisconsin	65,503	5,000,000	76	State (U.S.) ... D	Madison	English
Wyoming	97,818	462,000	4.7	State (U.S.) ... D	Cheyenne	English
Xinjiang Uygur (Sinkiang)	617,764	15,755,000	26	Autonomous region (China) ... D	Ürümqi	Turkish dialects, Mongolian, Tungus, English
Xizang (Tibet)	471,045	2,235,000	4.7	Autonomous region (China) ... D	Lhasa	Tibetan dialects
† Yemen	203,850	12,215,000	60	Republic ... A	Şan'ā'	Arabic
Yugoslavia	39,449	10,670,000	270	Republic ... A	Belgrade (Beograd)	Serbo-Croatian
Yukon Territory	186,661	31,000	0.2	Territory (Canada) ... D	Whitehorse	English, Inuktitut, indigenous
Yunnan	152,124	38,450,000	253	Province (China) ... D	Kunming	Chinese (Mandarin), Tibetan dialects, Khmer, Miao-Yao
† Zaire	905,446	39,750,000	44	Republic ... A	Kinshasa	French, Kikongo, Lingala, Swahili, Tshiluba
† Zambia	290,586	8,475,000	29	Republic ... A	Lusaka	English, Tonga, Lozi, other indigenous
Zhejiang	39,305	43,150,000	1,098	Province (China) ... D	Hangzhou	Chinese dialects
† Zimbabwe	150,873	10,000,000	66	Republic ... A	Harare (Salisbury)	English, Shona, Sindebele
WORLD	57,900,000	5,477,000,000	95	...	...	...

† Member of the United Nations (1992).
... None, or not applicable.
(1) No permanent population.
(2) Bophuthatswana, Ciskei, Transkei, and Venda are not recognized by the United Nations.
(3) North Cyprus unilaterally declared its independence from Cyprus in 1983.
(4) Claimed by Argentina.
(5) Includes West Bank, Golan Heights, and Gaza Strip.
(6) Future capital.
(7) Claimed by Comoros.
(8) Comprises Ceuta, Melilla, and several small islands.

Map Symbols

The map is a unique means of recording and communicating geographic information. By reducing the world to a smaller scale and symbolizing reality, it enables us to see regions of the earth well beyond our ordinary range of vision. Thus, a map represents one of the most convenient, accurate, and effective ways to learn about size, distance, direction, and the geographic features of our planet.

An atlas is a collection of general reference maps and, whether readers are interested in the political boundaries of the Middle East or in the distribution of oil reserves, an atlas is an indispensable aid to understanding the many facets of our complex earth and the general course of world events.

Basic continental and regional coverage of the world's land area is provided by this atlas. The reference maps, preceded by a map of the world, follow a continental arrangement: Europe, Asia, Australia, Africa, North America, and South America.

Many of the symbols used are self-explanatory. A complete legend below provides a key to the symbols on the reference maps in this atlas.

The surface configuration of the earth is represented by hill-shading, which gives the three-dimensional impression of landforms. This terrain representation conveys a realistic and readily visualized impression of the surface.

If the world used one alphabet and one language, no particular difficulty would arise in understanding nonalphabetic languages. However, some of the nations of the world use nonalphabetic languages. Their symbols are transliterated into the Roman alphabet. In this atlas a "local-name" policy generally was used for naming cities and towns and all local topographic and water features. However, for a few major cities the Anglicized name was preferred and the local name given in parentheses, for instance, Moscow (*Moskva*), Vienna (*Wien*), Cologne (*Köln*). In countries where more than one official language is used, a name is in the dominant local language. The generic parts of local names for topographic and water features are self-explanatory in many cases because of the associated map symbols or type styles.

Map Symbols

CULTURAL FEATURES

Political Boundaries
- International
- Secondary: State, Provincial, etc.

Cities, Towns and Villages
(Not applicable to maps at 1:20,000,000 or smaller scale or to those with legend in map margin)
- PARIS — 1,000,000 and over
- Ufa — 500,000 to 1,000,000
- Győr — 50,000 to 500,000
- Agadir — 25,000 to 50,000
- Moreno — 0 to 25,000
- TŌKYŌ — National Capitals
- Boise — Secondary Capitals

Transportation
- Railroads
- Railroad Ferries
- Caravan Routes

Other Cultural Features
- Dams
- Pipelines
- Pyramids
- Ruins

LAND FEATURES
- △ Peaks, Spot Heights
- = Passes

WATER FEATURES

Lakes and Reservoirs
- Fresh Water
- Fresh Water: Intermittent
- Salt Water
- Salt Water: Intermittent

Other Water Features
- Swamps
- Glaciers
- Rivers
- Canals
- Aqueduct — Aqueducts
- Ship Channels
- Falls
- Rapids
- Springs
- Water Depths
- Sand Bars
- Reefs

POLITICAL

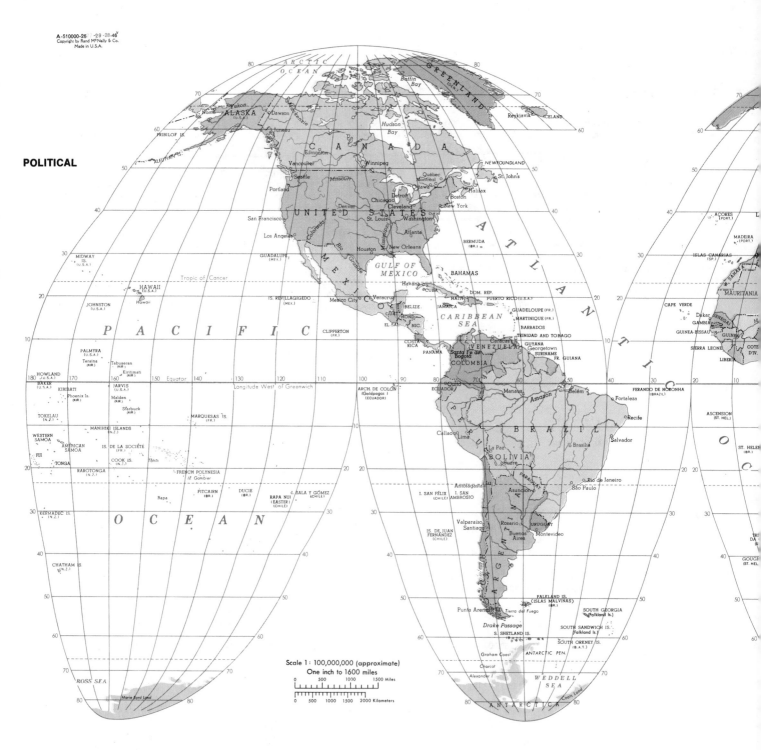

Scale 1 : 100,000,000 (approximate)
One inch to 1600 miles

0   500   1000   1500 Miles

0   500 1000 1500 2000 Kilometers

Comparative Land Areas (Land and inland water. Numbers indicate thousands of square miles.)

| CHINA 3,690 | INDIA 1,237 | KAZAKHSTAN 1,049 | SAUDI ARABIA 830 | INDONESIA 752 | IRAN 632 | MONGOLIA 605 | PAKISTAN 340 | TURKEY 301 | MYANMAR 261 | ALL OTHERS 2,575 | RUSSIA 5,065 | 1,527 | ALL OTHERS 2,301 | SUDAN 968 | ALGERIA 920 | ZAIRE 905 | LIBYA 679 | CHAD 496 | NIGER 489 | ANGOLA 481 | MALI 479 | ETHIOPIA 447 | SOUTH AFRICA 434 | MAURITANIA 396 | EGYPT 387 |

— ASIA 17,300 — EUROPE 3,800 — AFRICA 11,700 —

Comparative Populations (Numbers indicate millions of people.) 1/1/92 estimate

| CHINA 1,181.6 | INDIA 874.1 | INDONESIA 195.3 | JAPAN 124.3 | PAKISTAN 119.0 | BANGLADESH 118.0 | VIETNAM 68.3 |

— ASIA 3,331.5 —

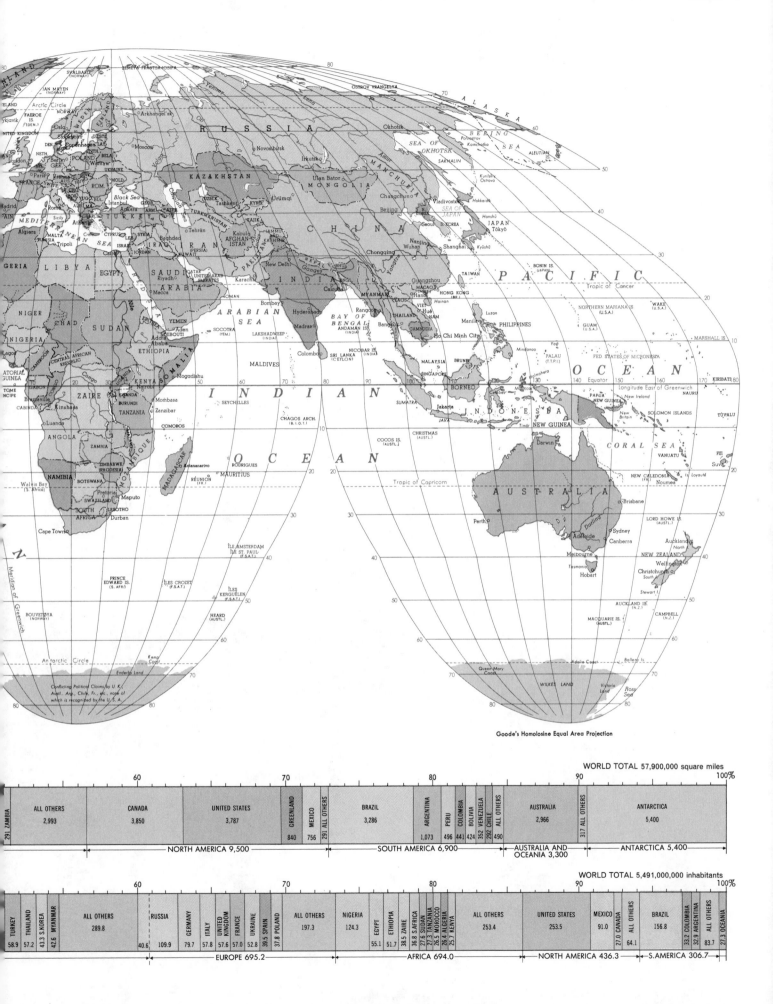

Goode's Homolosine Equal Area Projection

Conflicting Political Claims by U.K., Austl., Arg., Chile, Fr., etc., none of which is recognized by the U.S.A.

WORLD TOTAL 57,900,000 square miles

Region	Country	Value
	ZAMBIA	291
	ALL OTHERS	2,993
	CANADA	3,850
NORTH AMERICA 9,500	UNITED STATES	3,787
	GREENLAND	840
	MEXICO	756
	ALL OTHERS	291
	BRAZIL	3,286
	ARGENTINA	1,073
	PERU	496
	COLOMBIA	441
SOUTH AMERICA 6,900	BOLIVIA	424
	VENEZUELA	352
	CHILE	292
	ALL OTHERS	490
AUSTRALIA AND OCEANIA 3,300	AUSTRALIA	2,966
	ALL OTHERS	317
ANTARCTICA 5,400	ANTARCTICA	5,400

WORLD TOTAL 5,491,000,000 inhabitants

Region	Country	Value
	TURKEY	58.9
	THAILAND	57.2
	S.KOREA	43.3
	MYANMAR	42.6
	ALL OTHERS	289.8
EUROPE 695.2	RUSSIA	109.9
		40.6
	GERMANY	79.7
	ITALY	57.8
	UNITED KINGDOM	57.6
	FRANCE	57.0
	UKRAINE	52.8
	SPAIN	39.5
	POLAND	37.8
	ALL OTHERS	197.3
	NIGERIA	124.3
	EGYPT	55.1
	ETHIOPIA	51.7
	ZAIRE	38.5
	S.AFRICA	36.8
AFRICA 694.0	SUDAN	27.6
	TANZANIA	27.3
	MOROCCO	26.5
	ALGERIA	26.4
	KENYA	25.7
	ALL OTHERS	253.4
	UNITED STATES	253.5
NORTH AMERICA 436.3	MEXICO	91.0
	CANADA	27.0
	ALL OTHERS	64.1
	BRAZIL	156.8
S.AMERICA 306.7	COLOMBIA	33.2
	ARGENTINA	32.9
	ALL OTHERS	83.7
	OCEANIA	27.3

40,000 SQ MI
AREA

0   100   200

Miles

**Cities,
Towns,
and
Villages**

0 to 25,000 ○   100,000 to 250,000 ◉   1,000,000 and over ◉

25,000 to 100,000 •   250,000 to 1,000,000 ◎   Major urbanized area

0   50   100   200   300   400   500 Miles

0   100   200   300   400   500   600   800 Kilometers

Longitude West of Greenwich   Longitude East of Greenwich

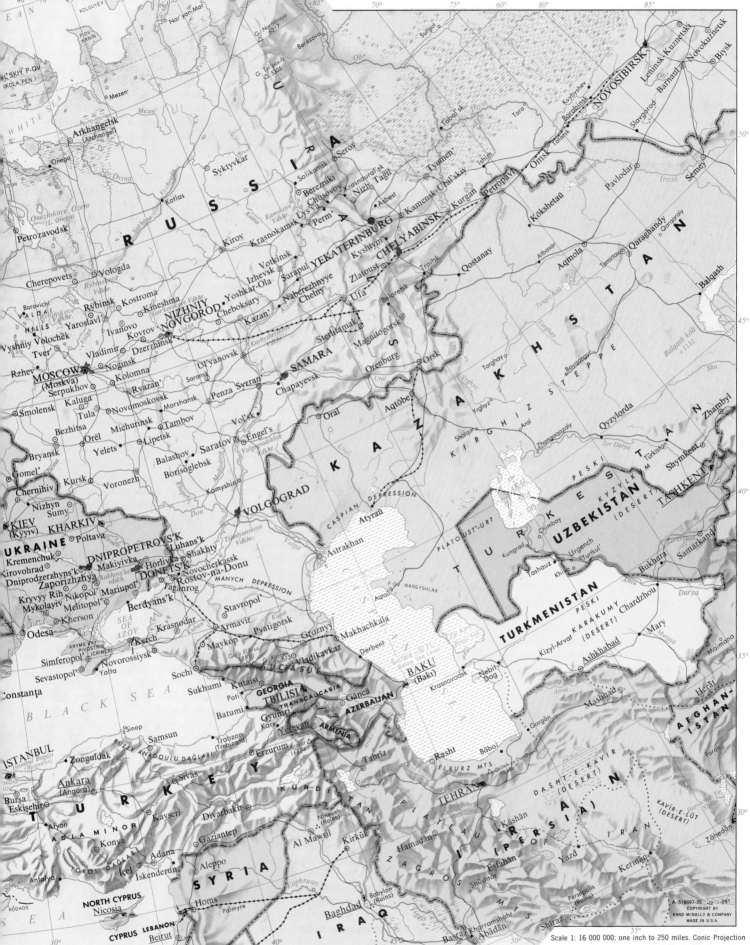

Scale 1: 16 000 000; one inch to 250 miles. Conic Projection

Elevations and depressions are given in feet

A-519697-26
COPYRIGHT BY
RAND McNALLY & COMPANY
MADE IN U.S.A.

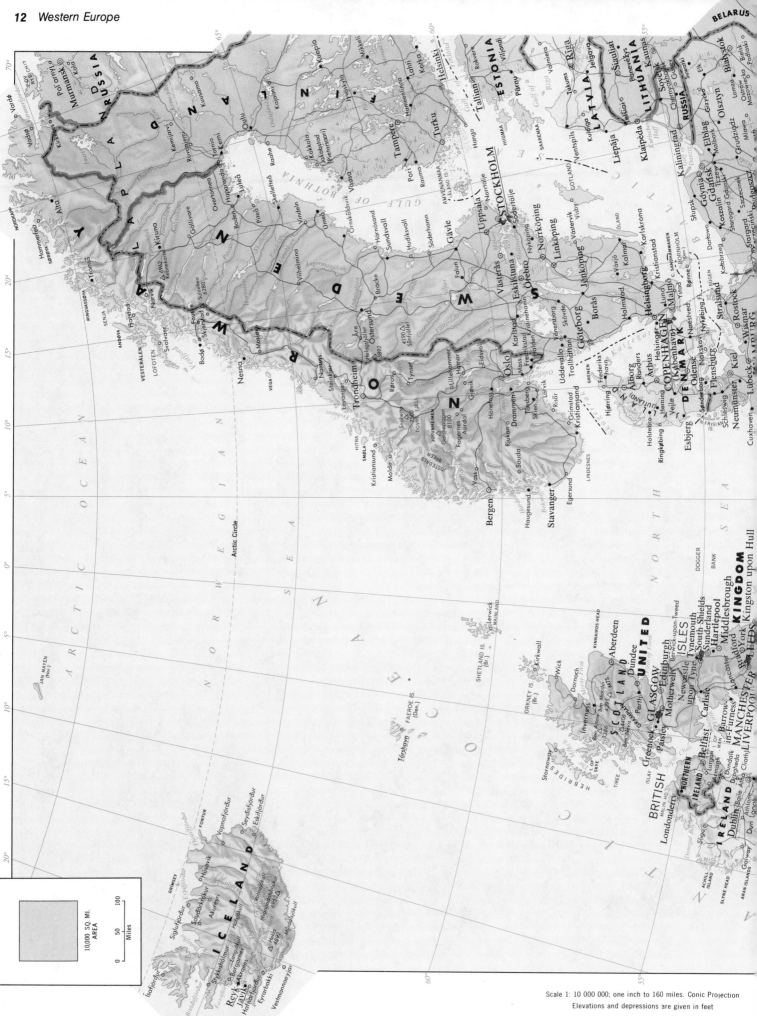

Scale 1: 10 000 000; one inch to 160 miles. Conic Projection
Elevations and depressions are given in feet

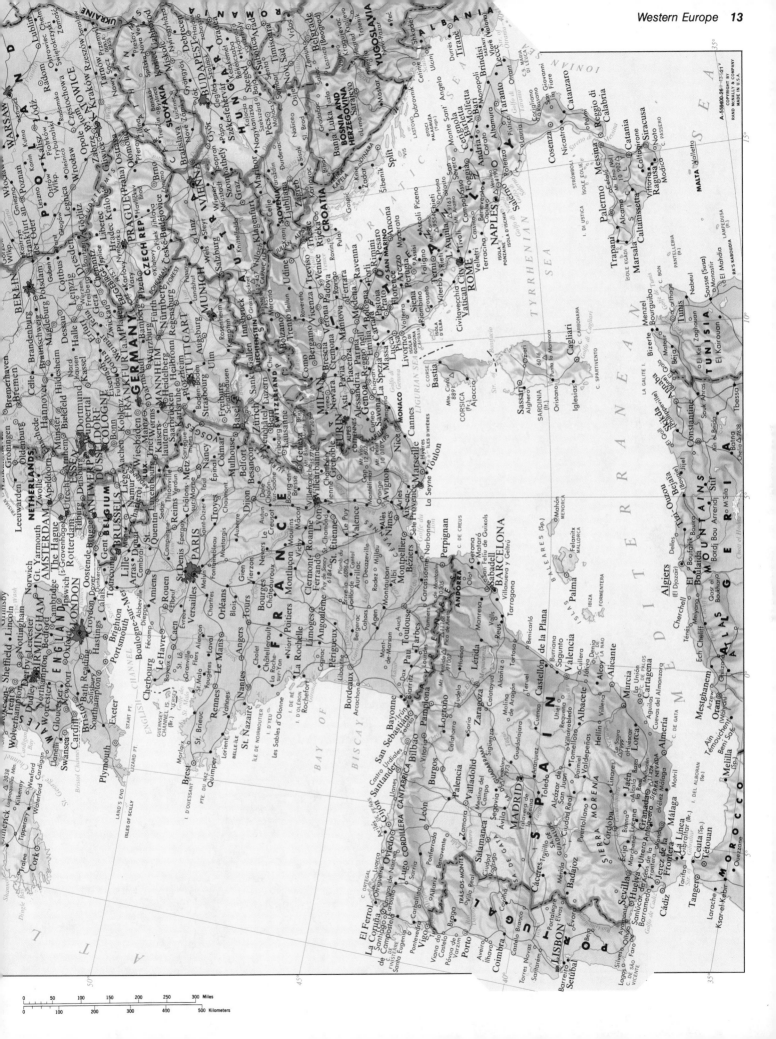

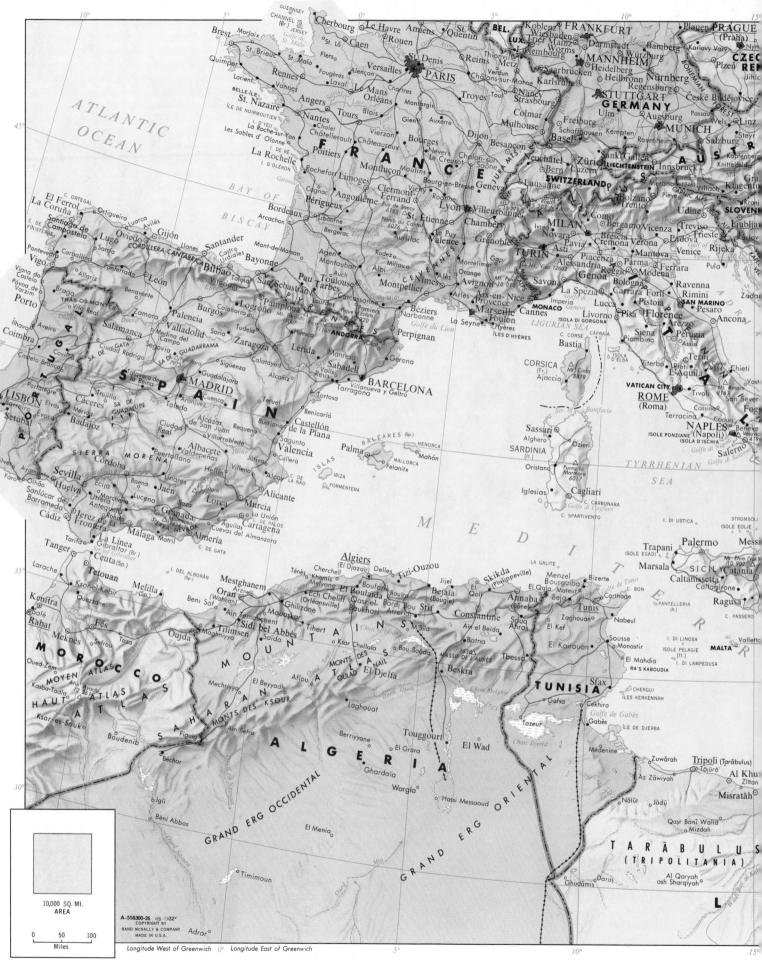

10,000 SQ. MI.
AREA

0   50   100
Miles

A-558300-26
COPYRIGHT BY
RAND McNALLY & COMPANY
MADE IN U.S.A.

Longitude West of Greenwich   0°   Longitude East of Greenwich

Scale 1:10 000 000; one inch to 160 miles. Bonne's Projection
Elevations and depressions are given in feet

The Turkish Republic of Northern Cyprus
unilaterally declared its independence
on Nov. 15, 1983.

Areas occupied by Israel since 1967.

Cities, Towns, and Villages			
0 to 25,000 ○	100,000 to 250,000 ◉	1,000,000 and over ◉	
25,000 to 100,000 •	250,000 to 1,000,000 ◎	Major urbanized area	

Scale 1:20 000 000; one inch to 315 miles.
Lambert's Azimuthal, Equal Area Projection
Elevations and depressions are given in feet

40,000 SQ. MI.
AREA

0   150   300
Miles

OCEAN

SEVERNAYA ZEMLYA
(NORTHERN LAND)

VRANGELYA
(WRANGEL)

M. CHELYUSKIN

CHUKOTSKOYE NAGORYE

Arctic Circle

KORYAKSKIY KHREBET

TAYMYR
BYRRANGA

LAPTEV SEA

EAST SIBERIAN SEA

DE LONGA

NOVAYA SIBIR

KOTEL'NYY
NOVOSIBIRSKIYE O-VA
(NEW SIBERIAN ISLANDS)
MALYY LYAKHOVSKIY
LYAKHOVSKIY

M. SHELAGSKIY

AYON

MEDVEZH'I

Ambarchik

Markovo

Anadyr

Anadyrskiy Zaliv

M. OLYUTORSKIY

KARAGIN

P-OV
GORY

BOL'SHOY
BEGICHEV

Nordvik

Tiksi

Taymyr

Khatangskiy
Zaliv

M. SVYATOY
NOS

M. BUOR-
KHAYA

Yana

Kazach ye

KHREBET

Nizhne Kolymsk

Srednekolymsk

Zyryanka

Grizhiga

Penzhino

Tilichiki

M. KAMCHATSKIY

P-OV

Khatanga

Bulun

Ust'-Olenek

Zhigansk

Abyy

Verkhoyansk

CHERSKOGO

KHREBET GYDAN (KOLYMSKIY)

Gora Chen
10171

Magadan

M. TAYGONOS

Yomsk

M. ALEVINA

KAMCHATKA

Klyuchevskaya sop.
15 584

Petropavlovsk-
Kamchatskiy

Noril'sk

GORY
PUTORANA

Turukhansk

arka

Olenek

Zashiversk

VERKHOYANSKIY KHREBET

Aldan

Oymyakon

 Okhotsk

Verkhne-Kamchatsk

Ust'-Bol'sheretsk

Tura

Nizhnyaya Tunguska

Vilyuysk

Suntar

Yakutsk

Aldanskaya

Amga

Ust'-Maya

DZHUGDZHUR KHREBET

Nel'kan

Ayan

SHANTAR

Chumikan

M. YELIZAVETY

Okha

SAKHALIN

SEA OF OKHOTSK

Yartsevo

G. Polkan
3543

Baykit

Podkamennaya Tunguska

Peleduy

Vitim

Mukhtuya

Olekminsk

Tommot

Aldan

Aleksandrovsk

Yeniseysk

Ilimsk

Kirensk

GOLETS-
PURPULA
5377

PATOM
PLATEAU

Bodaybo

GOLETS-
SKALISTYY
9180

STANOVOY KHREBET

Nel'kan

Udskaya Guba

Chumikan

TERPENIYA

Poronaysk

Uglegorsk

Yuzhno-Sakhalinsk

TSK Krasnoyarsk

Bogotol

Kansk

Tayshet

Bratsk

Nizhne-Angarsk

Piramida
10801

Tulun

Kutulik

Bratskoye
Vdkhr.

Oz. Baykal
(Lake Baikal)

Barguzin

Surface elev.1535 Ft.
above sea level

VILYUY

Tyndinskiy

Skovorodino

Zeya

Nerchinsk

Nerchinskiy
Zavod

Belogorsk

Svobodnyy

Nikolayevsk-na-Amure

KHREBET BUREINSKIY

Komsomol'sk
na-Amure

Sovetskaya
Gavan

Malmyzh

Tatar Strait

Kholmsk

Korsakov

N'

Balakhta

Nizhneudinsk

Zhigalovo

Kachuga

BAYKAL'SKIY KHREBET

Sretensk

Amur

Blagoveshchensk

Ust' Tyrma

Bureya

Birobidzhan

Khabarovsk

Wakkanai

HOKKAIDŌ

Otaru

Sapporo

znetski

Minusinsk

Abakan

KHREBET

Cheremkhovo

Munku
Sardyk
11457

Angarsk

Irkutsk

Kyren

Ulan-Ude

NERCHINSKIY KHREBET

Chita

Nerchinsk

YABLONOVYY KHREBET

Goukou

Nenjiang

Dalnerechensk

Spassk-
Dal'niy

Ussuriysk

Artem

Nakhodka

Vladivostok

SAYAN

Kyzyl

TANNU-OLA

Petrovsk-Zabaykal'skiy
Goradakan

Kyakhta

Aginskoye

Aksha

Borzya

Onon

Kerulen

LESSER
KHINGAN
RANGE

Qiqihar

Hailun

Suihua

Boli

Mudanjiang

Yanji

USSURIYSKIY KHREBET
SIKHOTE ALIN

Nojin

Chongjin

Har-us Nuur

Hövd

HANGAYN NURUU
KHANGAI MTS.

Uliastay

Khövsgöl
Nuur

Selenge

Ulan Bator
(Ulaanbaatar)

Öndörhaan

GREATER KHINGAN RANGE

Wenquan

Fuyu

Tao'an

Jarud Qi

Shuangliao

Jilin

Dunhua

Hunchun

Najin

SEA OF JAPAN

HONSHŪ

Kanazawa

Taast Bogd
13419

MONGOLIA

Sayr Usa

CHINA

Chifeng

Changchun

MANCHURIA

HARBIN

Jilin

Fushun

SHENYANG

NORTH
KOREA

P'yongyang

Matsue

Tottori

KYOTO

KOBE

OSAKA

Okayama

Kōchi

GOBI OR SHAMO
(DESERT)

Weichang

Chongde

Kaesŏng

SOUTH
KOREA

SEOUL

Hiroshima

PUSAN

Taegu

Hami

Zhangjiakou

Fengzhen

BEIJING

TIANJIN

Lüshun

Dalian

Korea Bay

YELLOW SEA

SHANDONG BANDAO

Andong

Korea Strait

Tsushima

Longitude East of Greenwich

90°   100°   110°   120°

Baoding

Bo
Hai

A-570000-26 -1514-33
COPYRIGHT BY
RAND McNALLY & COMPANY
MADE IN U.S.A.

0   100   200   300   400   500   600 Miles

0   200   400   600   800   1000 Kilometers

40,000 SQ MI
AREA

0   300   600
Miles

A-519695-26   11-19-15-36PP
COPYRIGHT BY
RAND MCNALLY & COMPANY
MADE IN U.S.A.

Longitude East of Greenwich

Scale 1:40 000 000; one inch to 630 miles. Lambert's Azimuthal, Equal Area Projection
Elevations and depressions are given in feet

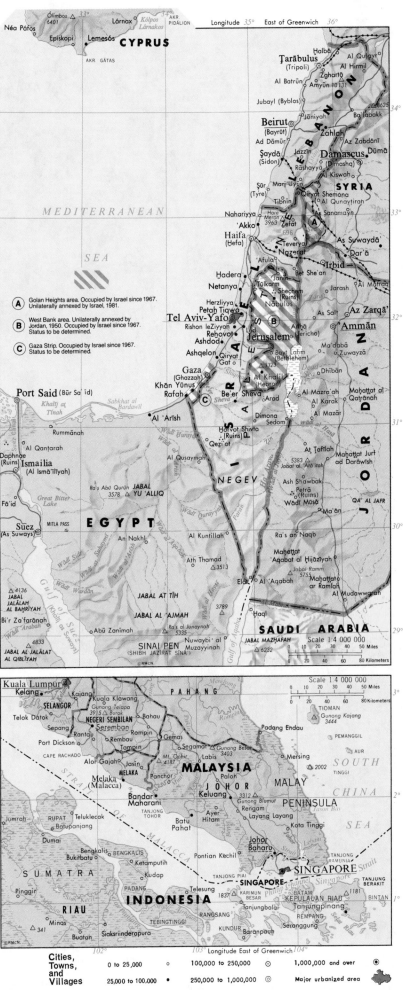

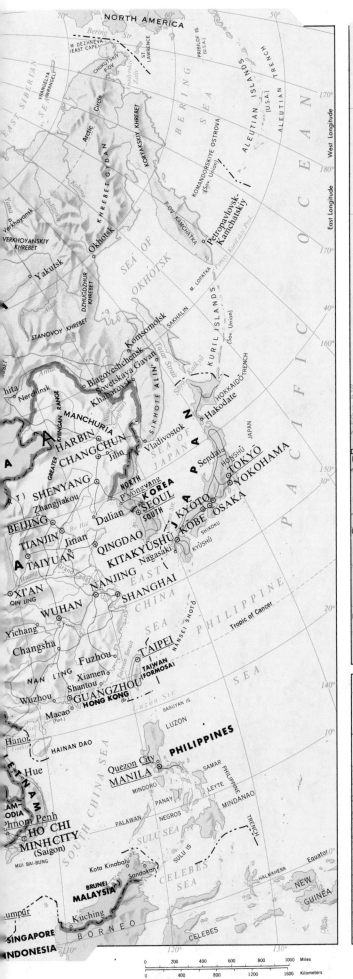

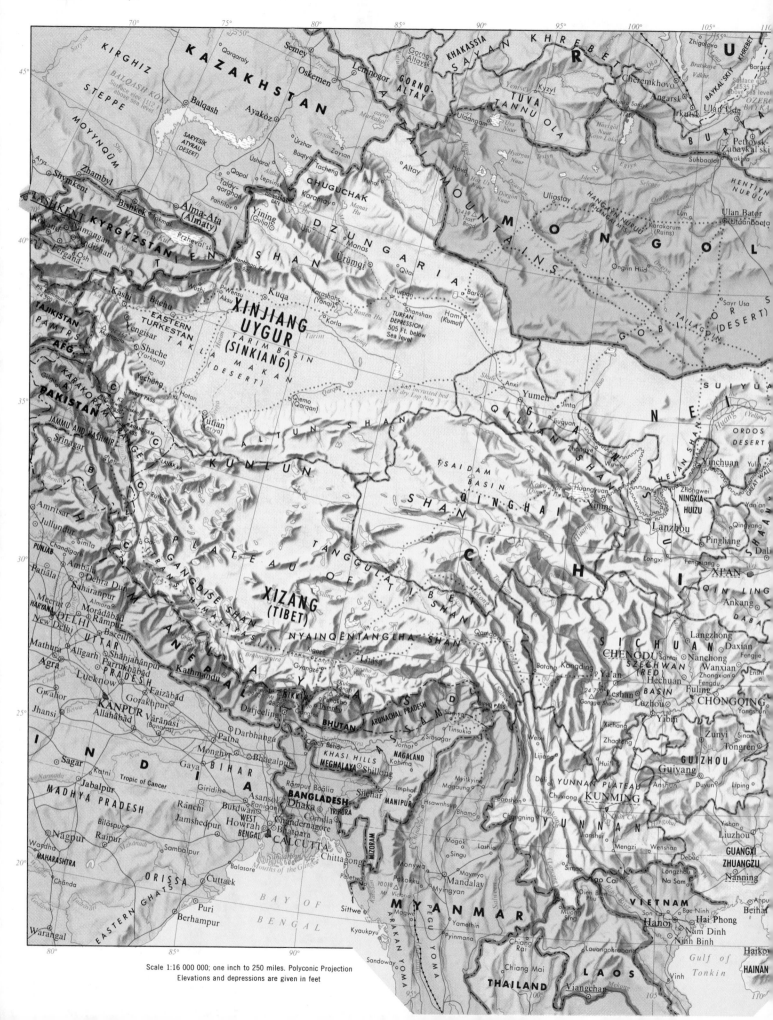

Scale 1:16 000 000; one inch to 250 miles. Polyconic Projection
Elevations and depressions are given in feet

Chinese Provinces, Autonomous Regions (AR) and Municipalities (M)

Conventional Form — Pinyin Form

Conventional Form	Pinyin Form
Anhwei	Anhui
Chekiang	Zhejiang
Fukien	Fujian
Heilungkiang	Heilongjiang
Honan	Henan
Hopeh	Hebei
Hunan	Hunan
Hupeh	Hubei
Inner Mongolia (AR)	Nei Monggol
Kansu	Gansu
Kiangsi	Jiangxi
Kiangsu	Jiangsu
Kirin	Jilin
Kwangsi (AR)	Guangxi Zhuangzu
Kwangtung	Guangdong
Kweichow	Guizhou
Liaoning	Liaoning
Ningsia Hui (AR)	Ningxia Huizu
Peking (M)	Beijing
Shanghai (M)	Shanghai
Shansi	Shanxi
Shantung	Shandong
Shensi	Shaanxi
Sinkiang (AR)	Xinjiang Uygur
Szechwan	Sichuan
Tibet (AR)	Xizang
Tientsin (M)	Tianjin
Tsinghai	Qinghai
Yunnan	Yunnan

A — Area occupied by Pakistan and claimed by India.

B — Area claimed and occupied by India; status disputed by Pakistan.

C — Area occupied by China and claimed by India.

D — Area occupied by India and claimed by China.

Habomai, Shikotan, Kunashiri, and Etorofu, occupied since 1945, are claimed by Japan pending a final peace treaty.

40,000 SQ MI AREA

0   100   200
Miles

Longitude East of Greenwich

0   50   100   200   300   400   500 Miles

0   100   200   400   600   800 Kilometers

A-569700-26   -14 11-26 VP
COPYRIGHT BY
RAND McNALLY & COMPANY
MADE IN U.S.A.

40,000 SQ MI
AREA

0   100   200
Miles

A-569400-26 -20-17-36
COPYRIGHT BY
RAND McNALLY & COMPANY
MADE IN U.S.A.

Scale 1:16 000 000; one inch to 250 miles. Polyconic Projection
Elevations and depressions are given in feet

Longitude East of Greenwich

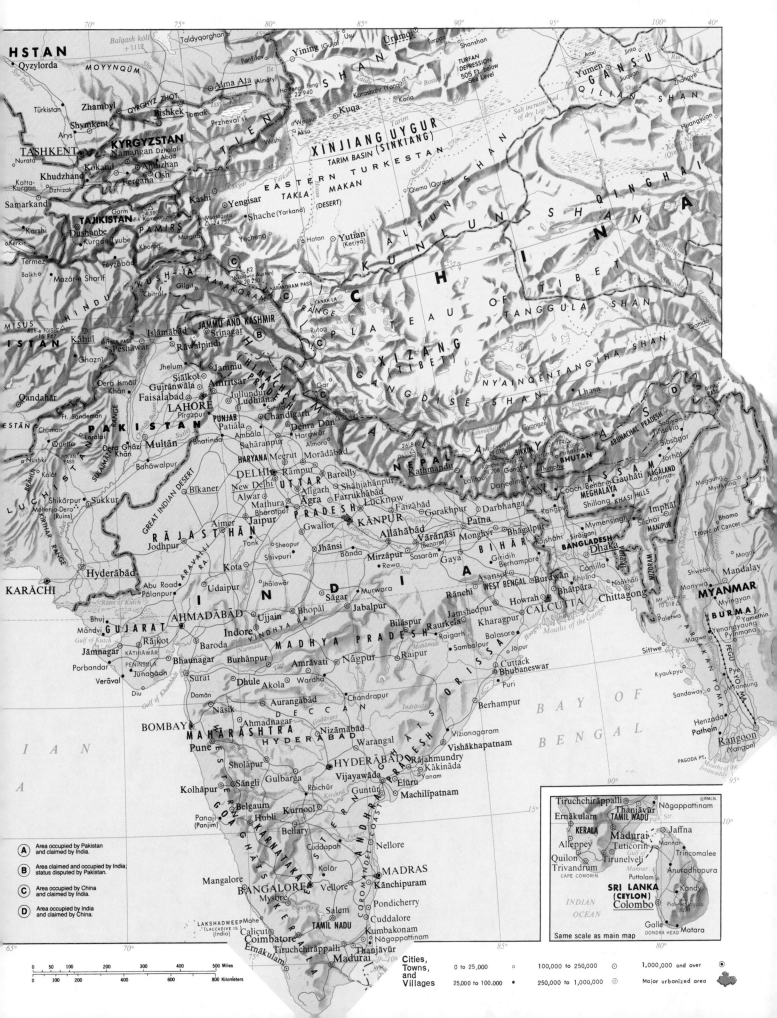

Cabugao   Iguig
Tuguegarao

120° 122°

Vigan   Bangued   Lubuagan
Narvacan   Divilacan Bay
Candon   Cabagan   PALANAN PT.
Bontoc   Ilagan   Palanan Bay
Cervantes   Mt. Amuyao   Cauayan
8799   Santiago   Echague
Luna   Jones

Mt. Pulog   Bagabag   SIERRA
San Fernando S. Juan   9612   Bayombong
Bauang   Aringay 7388   Baguio   Bambang
Bolinao   CABARRUYAN   Solano   Dupax   DIJOHAN PT.
Bani   Lingayen   San Fabian   Bambang   Casiguran
Agno   Alaminos   Gulf   Dagupan S. Nicolas
Burgos   Lingayen   Urdaneta S. Quintin   CAPE SAN ILDEFONSO
CAIMAN PT.   San Carlos   Tayug   16°
Dasol Bay   Infanta   Bayambang Rosales   Baler Bay
Santa Cruz   Mangatarem   Munoz   San Jose   Dingalan Bay
Candelaria   Camiling   Gerona   Victoria   Baler CAPE ENCANTO
High Pk.   Tarlac   Cabanatuan
6683   Paluig   LUZON   PHILIPPINES   SEA
Iba   Concepcion   Gapan
Pinatubo   S. Miguel   POLILLO IS.
5771   Angeles   Arayat   POLILLO
S. Narciso   Guagua   S. Fernando   Infanta Polillo   Patnanongan JOMALIG
S. Antonio   Subic   Malolos
Olongapo   Orani   Sta.   CALAGUAS ISLAND
SAMPALOC PT.   Balanga   Maria   BALESIN
Orion   Malabon   Quezon   Lamon Bay   Capalonga   Paracale
Mariveles   MANILA   City   Pasig   CABALETE   Labo   Talisay
CORREGIDOR ISLAND   Cavite   Laguna   Sta. Cruz   Mauban ALABAT   Daet
Naic   Silang Calamba   Nagcarlan   Mt. Labo   14°
Nasugbu   S. Pablo Atimonan   5066   San
Balayan   Lipa   7177 Mt. Banahao   Gumaca   Miguel   Lagonay
CABRA ISLAND   Lemery   Rosario   Lucena   Unisan   Macalelon   Mt. Isarog   Bay   Naga
Lubang   Batangas   Loba   Tayabas Bay   S. Narciso 6450   Pili   Bubi
LUBANG   AMBIL   Catanauan   Ragay   Baao
IS.   ISLAND   Paluan   Boac   S. Cruz   Ragay Gulf   Polangui Mayon
GOLD   Balanay   MARICABAN   Calapan   MARINDUQUE   Gulf   Volcano 8077
ISLAND   Bay   Verde I. Passage   ISLAND   Ligao
CAPE CALAVITE   VERDE   Naujan   Gasan   Torrijos   San Pascual   BURIAS   Legazpi
Mamburao   Mt. Halcon   MINDORO   DUMALI PT.   Pinamalayan   Jones   TICAO
8471   ISLAND
MINDORO   Banton   SIBUYAN   S. Jacinto
Sablayan   Mt. Baco   BANTON   ROMBLON ISLAND   Aroroy
8163   Romblon   MASBATE
DONGON PT.   Knob Pk.   TABLAS   Masbate
Scale 1:4 000 000   3031   Odiongan   SIBUYAN
S. Jose   Bulalacao   TABLAS   SEA
10 20 30 40 Miles   Looc   Busuanga
0 10 20 30 40 50 60 Kilometers   ILIN ISLAND   TARA
©RMCN

125°   130°   135°

PHILIPPINE   20°

PHILIPPINE
SEA   16°

PHILIPPINES
CATANDUANES
ISLAND
Legazpi   15°
Sorsogon
Catbalogan   SAMAR
Tacloban
Cebu   LEYTE   PHILIPPINE
DINAGAT ISLAND
34 578
SEA   10°
BOHOL
Mindanao
Sea   TRENCH
zamiz   Butuan
Cagayan
MINDANAO
otabato   Mt. Apo   Davao
9692   Davao Gulf   PALAU IS.
(T.T.P.I.)   5°
PULAU MIANGAS   SONSOROL
ISLANDS

Manado   KEPULAUAN   0°
TALAUD   Equator

Tondano   MUSSAU
Ternate   HALMAHERA   KEPULAUAN   NINIGO GROUP   ADMIRALTY ISLANDS   ISLAND
Laut   PULAU   MAPIA   HERMIT IS.   EMIRA
Maluku   MOROTAI   PULAU   ISLAND
(Molucca Sea)   SIAU   WAIGEO   MANUS   NEW HANOVER
PULAU   BIAK   ISLAND   Kavieng
Labuha   OBI   Sorong   Manokwari   PULAU YAPEN   BISMARCK
KEPULAUAN   PULAU   SALAWATI   JAZIRAH   PULAU   Namatanai
BANGGAI   TALIBU   DOBERAI   NUMFOOR   MUSSAU   Rabaul
PULAU   PULAU   SELAT DAMPIER   Jayapura   WITU   ARCH.   Kokopo
MANGOLE   MISOOL   Teluk Berau   (Sukarnapura)   ISLANDS
KEPULAUAN   PULAU OBI   Teluk   Aitape   NEW
SULA   PULAU SANANA   (MOLUCCAS)   Cenderawasih   Wewak   IRELAND
CERAM   PULAU ADI   PEGUNUNGAN VAN REES   Sepik   LONG ISLAND   NEW BRITAIN
(SERAM)   Fakfak   KARKAR ISLAND
Piru   PULAU AMBON   Kaimana   PEGUNUNGAN   Madang   Talasea   The Father
Ambon   Bula   MAOKE   Puncak Jaya Puncak Trikora   NEW GUINEA   Mt. Wilhelm 14 793   7546
BURU   PULAU   16 503 15 584   Mt. Giluwe 14 330   Lae
KEPULAUAN   BANDA   Mt. Bangeta   NEW BRITAIN
Manui   KEPULAUAN   PAPUA   13 520   NEW BRITAIN
Wowoni   TUKANGBESI   LUCIPARA   KEPULAUAN KAI   Dobo   NEW GUINEA   Morobe   TRENCH
LAUT BANDA   KAI KECIL   Huon Gulf
(BANDA SEA)   KEPULAUAN   Mt. Albert Edward   TROBRIAND IS.
ARU   13 090
PULAU   PULAU   YAMDENA   PULAU   OWEN STANLEY RA.
WETAR   DAMAR   KEPULAUAN   TRANGAN   ARAFURA   Merauke   Buna
PULAU   TANIMBAR   TANJUNG VALS   SEA   WOODLARK
ALOR   PULAU   PULAU   Port Moresby   ISLAND
Dili   MOA   SELARU   Mt. Victoria   D'ENTRECASTEAUX IS.
PANTAR   BABAR   PULAU   T3 208
I. DE ATAÚRO   YOS   Daru
TIMOR   SUDARSA   Torres   GREAT   CORAL   Samarai
Kupang   C. YORK   Strait   BARRIER   SEA
TIMOR   MELVILLE   COBOURG   CROKER ISLAND   C. ARNHEM   CAPE   REEF
SEA   ISLAND   PEN.   WESSEL IS   YORK
BATHURST   Van   GREAT   PEN.   Gulf of   10°
ISLAND   Diemen Gulf   Gulf of Carpentaria
Darwin   AUSTRALIA

125°   130°   135°   140°   145°   150°

0 50 100   200   300   400   500 Miles
0   100   200   400   600   800 Kilometers

INDONESIA

Pasuruan
G. Mahameru 12 060
G. Raung 11 225
Singaraja
BALI
Rinjani 12 224
LOMBOK
SUMBAWA
Besar
Sumbawa
Raboo
FLORES
Waingapu
SAVU SEA
Lomblen Pantar
ALOR
Dili
TIMOR
SUMBA
SAWU
ROTI
Kupang

SUNDA ISLANDS

SUNDA STRAIT

SUNDA TRENCH

INDIAN

OCEAN

TIMOR SEA

ARAFURA SEA

SELARU

TANJUNG VALS

CAPE LONDONDERRY
Joseph Bonaparte Gulf
C. VAN DIEMEN
CROKER
Van Diemen Gulf
MELVILLE
BATHURST
Clarence Str.
Anson Bay
COBOURG PEN.
Darwin
ARNHEM LAND
WESSEL IS.
CAPE ARNHEM
Blue Mud Bay
GROOTE EYLANDT
GULF OF
Pine Creek
Katherine
Limmen Bight
CARPENTARIA
SIR EDWARD PELLEW GROUP
WELLESLEY IS.

Wyndham
Mt. Hann 2800
KING LEOPOLD RANGES
BUCCANEER ARCH.
CAPE LEVEQUE
DAMPIER LAND
Derby
Broome
GEIKIE RANGE
Fitzroy Crossing
Halls Creek
Stur Cr.
NORTHERN

Birdum
Victoria River Downs
Daly Waters
Borroloola
Newcastle Waters
Woods
Burketown
BARKLY TABLELAND
Alexandria
Dobbyn
Camooweal
TERRITORY
Tanami
Tennant Creek
Mount Isa
Malban
Duchess
Dajarra

LAGRANGE
EIGHTY MILE BEACH
LARREY POINT
RIPON
DAMPIER ARCH.
Port Hedland
DeGrey
Roebourne
MONTE BELLO IS.
BARROW
NORTH WEST CAPE
Marble Bar
Nullagine
GREAT SANDY DESERT
Mackay
Barrow Creek
Mt. Ziel 4955
MACDONNELL RANGES
Arltunga
Alice Springs
JAMES RANGE
QU
Macdonald

Millstream
HAMERSLEY RANGE
Onslow
Ashburton
Mt. Bruce 4024
Jiggalong
Disappointment
WESTERN
GIBSON DESERT
SIMPSON DESERT
Charlotte Waters
Birdsville
A

POINT CLOATES
Tropic of Capricorn
CAPE FARQUHAR
Carnarvon
Gascoyne
Peak Hill
Nabberu
Carnegie
Wells
Gillen
MUSGRAVE RANGES
Mt. Woodroffe 4970
EVERARD RANGES
The Alberga
Oodnadatta
E

BERNIER
DORRE
Shark Bay
DIRK HARTOG
STEEP POINT
Murchison
Meekatharra
Nannine
Cue
Mount Magnet
Sandstone
Austin
AUSTRALIA
Yeo
Laverton
STUART RANGE
William Creek
Eyre 39
Marree
Cooper's Cr.
Gregory

Ajana
HOUTMAN ROCKS
Northampton
Geraldton
Dongara
Mingenew
Moore
Barlee
Ballard
Menzies
Kalgoorlie
GREAT VICTORIA DESERT
SOUTH AUSTRALIA
Ooldea Station
Torrens
Farina
FLINDERS RANGES
Frome
Woomera
Pimba
Parachilna
SWANLAND
DARLING RANGE
Pithara
Miling
Moora
Lake Brown
Southern Cross
Coolgardie
Boulder
Goddard's Soak
Cowan
Norseman
Dundas
Rawlinna
Eucla
NULLARBOR PLAIN
Hughes
Penong
POINT FOWLER
Ceduna
EYRE PENINSULA
Gairdner
Everard
Peterborough
Whyalla
Port Pirie
Gladstone
Wallaroo
Moonta
Port Wakefield

Perth
Fremantle
Northam
York
Collie
Narrogin
Bunbury
Katanning
Ravensthorpe
Hopetoun
Esperance
Salmon Gums
ARCHIPELAGO OF THE RECHERCHE
GREAT AUSTRALIAN BIGHT
Port Lincoln
Gawler
Gulf St. Vincent
Adelaide
Murray Bridge
Murray

Geographe Bay
CAPE NATURALISTE
Busselton
CAPE LEEUWIN
Nornalup
Albany
King George Sd.
PT. D'ENTRECASTEAUX
WEST CAPE HOWE
KANGAROO
Encounter Bay
Naracoorte
Kingston
CAPE JAFFA
Mt. Gambier

INDIAN OCEAN

40,000 SQ MI AREA

0   100   200
Miles

A-590200 26 4 2-14
COPYRIGHT BY
RAND McNALLY & COMPANY
MADE IN U.S.A.

Longitude 115° East of Greenwich

Scale 1:16 000 000; one inch to 250 miles. Lambert's Azimuthal, Enual Area Projection
Elevations and depressions are given in feet

NEW GUINEA

PAPUA NEW GUINEA

Mt. Albert Edward △ 13 100
Mt. Victoria △
13 363
Port Moresby

Buna

OWEN STANLEY RA.

TROBRIAND IS.
WOODLARK

D'ENTRECASTEAUX
ISLANDS

CHOISEUL
VELLA
LAVELLA
RENDOVA
NEW
GEORGIA
SANTA ISABEL
RUSSELL IS.
FLORIDA
TULAGI
Honiara
GUADALCANAL

SOLOMON ISLANDS

MALAITA

SAN CRISTÓBAL

RENNELL

SANTA CRUZ
ISLANDS

SOUTH CAPE
Samarai
LOUISIADE
ARCHIPELAGO
TAGULA
ROSSEL

MULGRAVE
THURSDAY
BANKS
HORN
PRINCE OF
WALES
CAPE YORK

Torres Strait

Weipa
CAPE
YORK
PENINSULA

Normanton

Croydon

Forsayth

Mungana
ATHERTON
PLATEAU
△ 5287
Mt. Bartle Frere

Laura
Cooktown
Palmerville

CAPE MELVILLE

OSPREY REEF

CORAL SEA

HOLMES
REEFS

WILLIS IS.

TORRES IS.

BANKS
ISLANDS

ESPÍRITU SANTO
MAEWO

NEW
MALEKULA
AMBRIM
EPI

PENTECOST

HEBRIDES
VANUATU

EFATE
Port Vila

Richmond

Hughenden

Cairns
Ingham
HINCHINBROOK I.
Halifax Bay
Townsville
Bowen
WHITSUNDAY
CUMBERLAND IS.
Mackay
NORTHUMBERLAND IS.

FLINDERS
REEFS

TREGROSSE IS.

MARION REEF

LIHOU REEFS

PACIFIC

GREAT BARRIER REEF

CLARKE RA.
CONNORS RANGE
Mt. Dalrymple △
4190

SWAIN REEFS

WRECK REEFS

ÎLES CHESTERFIELD
(Fr.)

ÎLES BÉLEP

OUVÉA

ÎLES LOYAUTÉ
(French)
LIFOU
MARÉ

EROMANGA
TANA
ANEITYUM

Ioncurry

Kynuna

Winton

QUEENSLAND

GREAT

DIVIDING

Barcaldine
Jericho

Longreach

Yaraka

Blackall

BUCKLAND
TABLELAND

Clermont
Emerald
Dinga

RANGE

Rockhampton
Mount Morgan
CURTIS
Gladstone

NEW
CALEDONIA
(Fr.)
Nouméa

ÎLE DES PINS

Tropic of Capricorn

Windorah
Yamma Yamma

ARTESIAN

Quilpie

Charleville
Roma

Thargomindah

Cunnamulla

Hungerford

RANGE
GREY
RANGE

St. George
Dirranbandi

DARLING
DOWNS
Toowoomba
Ipswich
Warwick

Bundaberg
Hervey
Bay
SANDY CAPE
Maryborough
Gympie
Dalby
Brisbane
N. STRADBROKE I.
Southport

FRASER

OCEAN

160°
165°
170°

MAIN
BARRIER
RANGE

Broken Hill

Wilcannia

Brewarrina
Bourke

Cobar
Nyngan

Coonamble

Walgett

Moree
Narrabri
Capoompeta △
Glen Innes
Inverell △ 5100
NEW
ENGLAND
RANGE
△ 5300
The Round Mountain
Armidale

Tamworth
WARRUMBUNGLE
RA.
LIVERPOOL
RA.

Roberts
Lismore

Tenterfield △ 4495

Grafton

Kempsey

Port Macquarie

LORD HOWE I.
(NEW S. WALES)

NEW SOUTH WALES

MURRAY
RIVERINA
REGION

Renmark
Wentworth
Mildura
Peebinga

Swan Hill
Kerang

Yanac
Horsham
Echuca

Bendigo
VICTORIA
Ararat
Maryborough

Hamilton
Ballarat
Portland
Geelong
Warrnambool
CAPE OTWAY

Hay
Narrandera
Deniliquin
Albury

Wagga Wagga

Benalla
Mt. Kosciusko △
7310
SNOWY
MTS.

MELBOURNE

Wilcannia

West
Wyalong
Forbes
Bathurst
Orange
BLUE
MTS.

Dubbo

Cessnock
Maitland
Newcastle

SYDNEY
Botany Bay
Wollongong

Goulburn
Jervis Bay
Canberra
AUSTL. CAP. TER.
Cooma
GREAT
Bega
Bombala

CAPE HOWE

Wonthaggi
WILSON'S
PROMONTORY
NINETY MILE BEACH
Bairnsdale

KING I.

FLINDERS
FURNEAUX GROUP
CAPE BARREN

TASMAN

SEA

HUNTER IS.

TASMANIA
Burnie
Ulverstone
Mt. Ossa △
5305
Devonport
Launceston
Strahan
New Norfolk
Risdon
Hobart
BRUNY
SOUTH EAST CAPE

145°

150°

155°

160°

0   50 100   200   300   400   500 Miles
0   100   200   400   600   800 Kilometers

NEW ZEALAND (inset)

PACIFIC

OCEAN

NORTH CAPE
Kaitaia
Russell
Devonport
GREAT
BARRIER
Auckland
NORTH ISLAND Hamilton
Bay of
Plenty
EAST CAPE

North Taranaki Bight
New Plymouth
C. EGMONT
South Taranaki Bight

Ruapehu
Vol. △
9175
Wanganui

Gisborne

Napier
Hastings
Palmerston North

**NEW
ZEALAND**

CAPE
FAREWELL
Nelson
Tasman
Bay

Lower Hutt
Wellington

Cook
Strait

TASMAN

SEA

Karamea Bight

CAPE FOULWIND

Greymouth
Hokitika

SOUTH ISLAND
SOUTHERN ALPS
Mt.
Cook △
12 349

Pegasus Bay

Christchurch

CASCADE PT.

Canterbury Bight
Timaru

PACIFIC

RESOLUTION
ISLAND
Dunedin
CAPE SAUNDERS

Foveaux
Strait
Invercargill

STEWART ISLAND
SOUTHWEST
CAPE

34°

38°

42°

46°

168°
172°
176°
180°

Same scale as main map

©RMcN

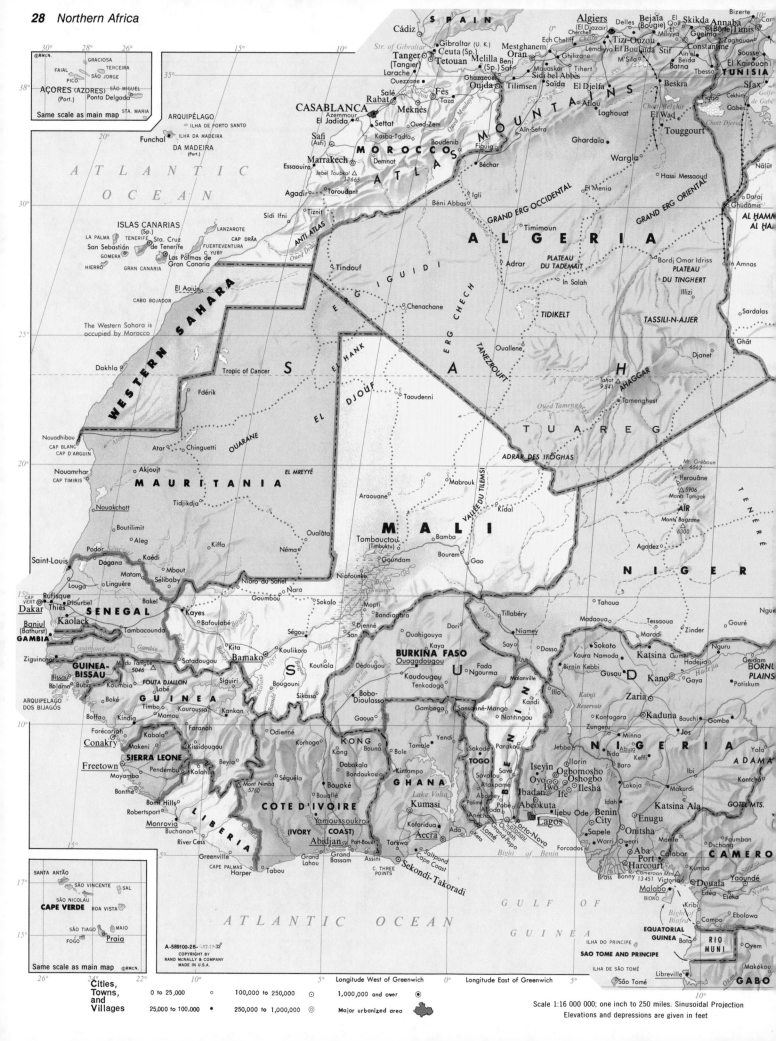

ATLANTIC OCEAN

AÇORES (AZORES)
(Port.)
Same scale as main map

GRACIOSA
TERCEIRA
FAIAL
SÃO JORGE
PICO
SÃO MIGUEL
Ponta Delgada
STA. MARIA

©RMCN.

SPAIN

Cádiz
Str. of Gibraltar
Gibraltar (U.K.)
Tanger (Tangier)
Ceuta (Sp.)
Melilla (Sp.)
Tetouan
Larache
Ouezzane

Algiers (El Djazair)
Delles
Bejaïa (Bougie)
Skikda
Annaba (Bône)
Bizerte
Tunis
TUNISIA
Sousse
Sfax

Ech Cheliff
Mestghanem
Oran
Sidi bel Abbès
Saïda
Tilimsen
Oujda
Taza
Fès
Meknès
Rabat
Salé
CASABLANCA
El Jadida
Settat
Oued-Zem
Kasba-Tadla
Safi (Asfi)
Marrakech
Demnat
Essaouira
Jebel Toubkal △ 13665
Agadir
Taroudant
Tiznit

MOROCCO
ATLAS MOUNTAINS

ALGERIA

Béchar
Figuig
Boudenib
Aïn-Sefra
Ghardaïa
Laghouat
Aflou
El Djelfa
Beskra
Batna
El Kairouan
El Wad
Touggourt
Wargla
Hassi Messaoud
El Menia
El Goléa

GRAND ERG OCCIDENTAL
GRAND ERG ORIENTAL

AL HAMM
AL HA

Ghudāmis
Darāj
Nālūt

Islas Canarias (Sp.)
LANZAROTE
FUERTEVENTURA
GRAN CANARIA
TENERIFE
LA PALMA
GOMERA
HIERRO
San Sebastián
Sta. Cruz de Tenerife
Las Palmas de Gran Canaria
CAP DRÂA
C. YUBY
Sidi Ifni

ANTI ATLAS

Béni Abbas
Igli
Timimoun
Adrar
In Salah
PLATEAU DU TADEMAÏT
Bordj Omar Idriss
PLATEAU DU TINGHERT
In Amnas
Illizi
Sardales
Ghât
Djanet

ATLANTIC OCEAN

Funchal
ILHA DA MADEIRA (Port.)
ARQUIPÉLAGO
ILHA DE PORTO SANTO
DA MADEIRA (Port.)

El Aaiún
CABO BOJADOR

WESTERN SAHARA
The Western Sahara is occupied by Morocco

Tropic of Cancer

Dakhla
Fdérik

S A H A R A
ERG IGUIDI
ERG CHECH
EL HANK
EL DJOUF
Chenachane
Ouallene
Taoudenni
TANEZROUFT
TIDIKELT
TASSILI-N-AJJER
Tahat △ 9541
AHAGGAR
Tamenghest
Oued Tamenghe

Nouadhibou
CAP BLANC
CAP D'ARGUIN

Atar
Chinguetti
OUARANE
EL MREYYÉ

Nouamrhar
CAP TIMIRIS

MAURITANIA
Akjoujt
Tidjikdja

Nouakchott

Boutilimit
Aleg
Kiffa
Néma
Oualâta

TUAREG
ADRAR DES IFÔGHAS
Mabrouk
VALLÉE DU TILEMSI
Kidal
Araouane
Bamba
Tombouctou (Timbuktu)
Bourem
Gao
Goundam
Niafounke
Débo

Mt. Grébour 6562
Iferouâne △5906
Monts Tamgak
AÏR
Monts Bagzane △6300
TÉNÉRÉ
Agadez

NIGER

Saint-Louis
Podor
Dagana
Louga
Linguère
Matam
Kaédi
Mbout
Sélibaby

SENEGAL
Dakar
CAP VERT
Rufisque
Thiès
Diourbel
Kaolack

Banjul (Bathurst)
GAMBIA
Ziguinchor

Bakel
Kayes
Bafoulabé
Kita
Satadougou
K_ta
Nioro du Sahel
Nara
Goumbou
Sokolo
Ségou
Djenné
San
Mopti
Bandiagara
Niamey
Tillabéry
Say
Dosso
Dori
Ouahigouya
Kaya
Madaoua
Tahoua
Tessaoua
Zinder
Gouré
Maradi
Birnin Kebbi
Sokoto
Kaura Namoda
Gusau
Katsina
Hadejia
Kano
Gumel
Geidam
BORNU PLAINS
Potiskum

GUINEA-BISSAU
Bissau
Bolama
Buba
Boké

FOUTA DJALLON
du Tamgue △5046

GUINEA
Labé
Timbo
Mamou
Kindia
Conakry
Forécariah

SIERRA LEONE
Makeni
Freetown
Moyamba
Bonthe

Siguiri
Kankan
Kouroussa
Faranah
Kabala
Kissidougou
Beyla
Odienné
Korhogo
Bouna
BURKINA FASO
Ouagadougou
Koudougou
Dédougou
Tenkodogo
Fada Ngourma
Koutiala
Sikasso
Bobo-Dioulasso
Bougouni
Gaoua
Gambaga
Sansanné-Mango
Natitingou
Kandi
Malanville
Illo
Kaïnji Reservoir
Zungeru
Kontagora
Zaria
Kaduna
Zungeru
Minna
Abuja
Jebba
Bida
Baro
Jos
Gombe
Bauchi
Keffi
Lokoja
Makurdi

NIGERIA

Kita
Bamako
Koulikoro

M A L I

B A N I

S E N E G A L

BURKINA FASO

S U D A N

Mont Nimba △5760
Bouaké
Séguéla
Bouaflé
KONG
Kong
Dabakala
Bondoukou
Tamale
Yendi
Sokodé
TOGO
GHANA
Kintampo
Kumasi
Koforidua
Accra
Tarkwa
Sekondi-Takoradi
Cape Coast
Saltpond
Ada
Lomé
Porto-Novo
Lagos
Abeokuta
Ibadan
Oyo
Iwo
Ife
Ilesha
Oshogbo
Ogbomosho
Iseyin
Benin City
Sapele
Warri
Forcados
Onitsha
Enugu
Owerri
Aba
Port Harcourt
Calabar
Katsina Ala
GOTEL MTS.
ADAMA
Yola
Kontcha
Ibi

COTE D'IVOIRE (IVORY COAST)
Yamoussoukro
Abidjan
Grand Bassam
Assini
C. THREE POINTS
Port-Bouet
Grand Lahou

LIBERIA
Monrovia
Buchanan
River Cess
Greenville
CAPE PALMAS
Harper
Tabou

Odienné
Man
Pendembu
Kolahun
Bomi Hills
Robertsport

Palimé
Anecho
Keta
Grand Popo
Abomey
Pobé
Ijebu Ode
Idah
Benin
Brass
Bonny
Cameroon Mtn 13451
Victoria
Bioko
Malabo
Douala
Yaoundé
Eséka
Kribi
Edéa
Campo
Ebolowa
Oyem
Makokou
Libreville

EQUATORIAL GUINEA
RIO MUNI
SAO TOME AND PRINCIPE
ILHA DO PRÍNCIPE
ILHA DE SÃO TOMÉ
São Tomé

CAMERO

GABO

Bight of Biafra

GULF OF GUINEA

ATLANTIC OCEAN

SANTA ANTÃO
SÃO VICENTE
SAL
SÃO NICOLAU
BOA VISTA
CAPE VERDE
SÃO TIAGO
MAIO
FOGO
Praia
Same scale as main map
©RMCN.

A-589100-26- 17-12 32
COPYRIGHT BY
RAND M^cNALLY & COMPANY
MADE IN U.S.A.

Cities, Towns, and Villages

0 to 25,000 ○	100,000 to 250,000 ⊙	1,000,000 and over ◉
25,000 to 100,000 •	250,000 to 1,000,000 ◎	Major urbanized area

Longitude West of Greenwich | Longitude East of Greenwich

Scale 1:16 000 000; one inch to 250 miles: Sinusoidal Projection
Elevations and depressions are given in feet

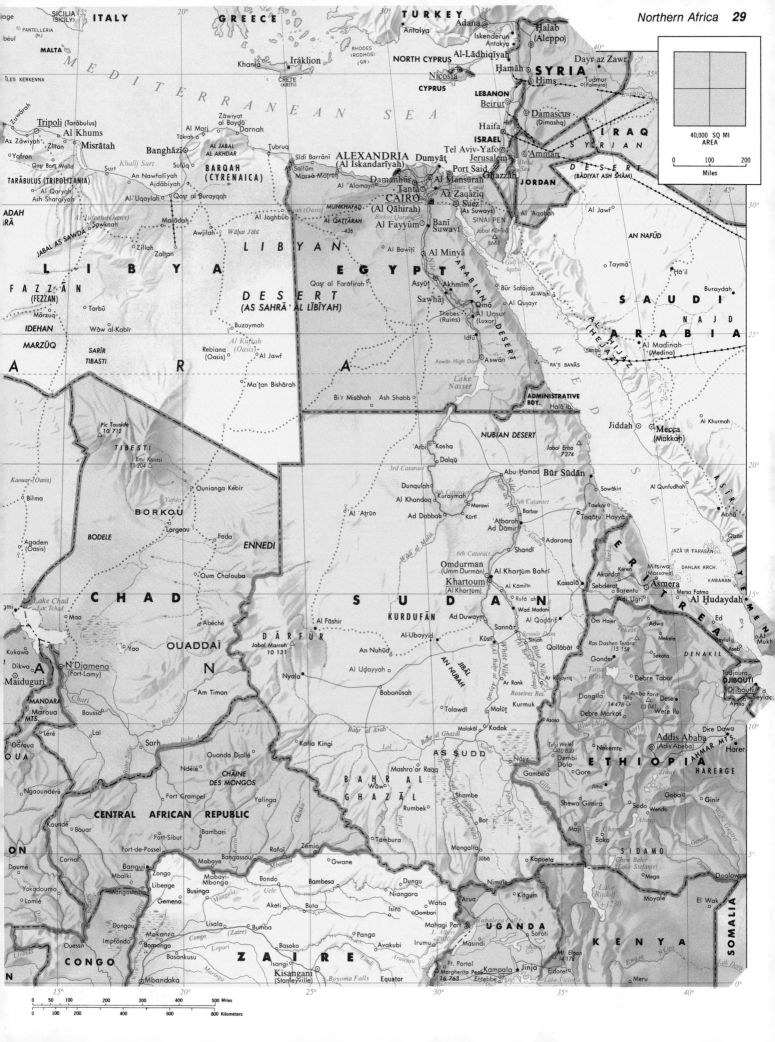

MEDITERRANEAN SEA

SICILIA (SICILY) ITALY
GREECE
TURKEY
Antalya
Adana
Halab (Aleppo)
PANTELLERIA (It.) béul
MALTA
RHODES (RODHOS) (GR)
Khaniá
Iráklion
CRETE (KRITI)
NORTH CYPRUS
Iskenderun
Al-Lādhiqīyah
Dayr az Zawr
ÎLES KERKENNA
Nicosia
CYPRUS
Ḩamāh
SYRIA
Tudmur (Palmyra)
Zuwārah
Tripoli (Tarābulus)
Az Zāwiyah
Al Khums
Misrātah
Al Marj
Darnah
Al JABAL AL AKHDAR
Sīdī Barrānī
ALEXANDRIA (Al Iskandarīyah)
Dumyāṭ
Port Said
Ḩims
LEBANON
Beirut
Damascus (Dimashq)
IRAQ
SYRIAN
Zliṭan
Yafran
Qaṣr Banī Walīd
Banghāzī
BARQAH (CYRENAICA)
Marsā Maṭrūḩ
Al ʿAlamayn
Damanhūr
Tanṭā
Al Manṣūrah
Az Zaqāzīq
Haifa
Tel Aviv-Yafo
Jerusalem
Ghazzah
Amman
DESERT (BĀDIYAT ASH SHĀM)
TARĀBULUS (TRIPOLITANIA)
Sūq
An Nawfalīyah
Ajdābiyah
Surt
Khalīj Surt
ISRAEL
JORDAN
Al ʿAqabah
Al Jawf
Al Qaryah
Ash Shargīyah
Al ʿUqaylah
Qaṣr al Burayqah
Suluq
Sīwah (Oasis)
MUNKHAFAḌ AL QAṬṬĀRAH -436
CAIRO (Al Qāhirah)
Al Fayyūm
Banī Suwayf
SINAI PEN
Jabal Kātrīnā 8668
AN NAFŪD
ADAH RĀ
Al Jufrah (Oasis)
Marādah
Al Jaghbūb
Awjilah
Wāḩat Jālū
LIBYAN
Al Bawīṭī
Al Minyā
Akhmīm
Būr Safājah
Al Wajh
Taymā
Hāʾil
Buraydah
JABAL AS SAWDĀ
Sawknah
Zillah
Zaltan
EGYPT
DESERT (AS SAHRĀʾ AL LĪBĪYAH)
Qaṣr al Farāfirah
Asyūṭ
Sawhāj
Qinā
Al Qusayr
Al Uqṣur (Luxor)
ARABIAN
SAUDI ARABIA
NAJD
FAZZĀN (FEZZAN)
Tarbū
Mārzuq
Wāw al-Kabīr
Buzaymah
Rebiana (Oasis)
Al Jawf
Thebes (Ruins)
Idfū
DESERT
Al Madīnah (Medina)
IDEHAN MARZŪQ
SARĪR TIBASTI
Maʿtan Bishārah
Aswān High Dam
Aswān
Lake Nasser
RAʾS BANĀS
AL HIJĀZ
Yanbū
AR
R
A
Bir Misāḩah
Ash Shabb
ADMINISTRATIVE BDY.
Halāʾib
Jiddah
Mecca (Makkah)
Al Khurmah
Pic Touside 10 712
TIBESTI
Emi Koussi 11 204
ʿArbi
Kosha
Dalqū
NUBIAN DESERT
Jabal Erba 7 274
Al Qunfudhah
Kaouar (Oasis)
Ounianga Kébir
Yarda
3rd Cataract
Dunqulah
Abu Ḩamad
Būr Sūdān
Sawākin
ASĪR
Abhā
Bilma
BORKOU
BODELE
Largeau
Fada
ENNEDI
Al Khandaq
Kuraymah
Marawi
4th Cataract
Al ʿAṭrūn
Ad Dabbah
Kūrtī
5th Cataract
Barbar
Tawkar
Taqāṭu Ḩayyā
JAZĀʾIR FARASĀN
Qizān
Agadem (Oasis)
Oum Chalouba
ʿAṭbarah
Ad Dāmir
Adarama
Shandī
ERITREA
Akordat
Keren
Mitsiwa (Massowa)
DAHLAK ARCH.
KAMARAN
YEMEN
Al Ḩudaydah
Lake Chad Lac Tchad
Mao
CHAD
6th Cataract
Omdurman (Umm Durmān)
Khartoum (Al Khartūm)
Al Khartūm Bahrī
Al Kāmilīn
SUDAN
Kassalā
Sebderat
Barentu
Adi Ugri
Asmera
Mersa Fatma
Ed
Kukawa
Dikwa
Maiduguri
MANDARA MTS.
N'Djamena (Fort-Lamy)
Mao
OUADDAÏ
Yao
Abéché
KURDUFĀN
Ad Duwaym
Rufaʿah
Wad Madanī
Ōm Hajer
Adwa
Mekele
Beylul
DENAKIL
Aseb
Al Mukh
Maroua
Bousso
Léré
Laï
DĀRFŪR
Jabal Marrah 10 131
Al Fāshir
An Nuhūd
Al-Ubayyid
Sannār
Kūstī
Sinjah
Sennār Dam
Qallābāt
Ras Dashen Terara 15 158
Gonder
Sekota
TIGRE
Garoua
Ngaoundéré
Nyala
Al Uḍayyah
Babanūsah
AN NUBAH
JIBĀL
White Nile (Al Bahr al Abyaḍ)
Ar Rank
Roseires Res.
Ar Ruṣayriṣ
Kurmuk
Dangila
Debre Tabor
Tana +6004
Amba Farit 14 478
Dese
Talo 13 041
Were Ilu
DJIBOUTI
Djibouti
Tadjoura
Aysha
Seylac
OUA
Am Timan
Talawdī
Malūṭ
Blue Nile (Al Bahr al Azraq)
Kurmuk
Asosa
Debre Markos
Dire Dawa
Harer
AHMAR MTS.
Ouanda Djallé
Ndélé
Fort Crampel
Yalinga
Kafia Kingi
BAHR AL GHAZĀL
Mashra ar Raqq
AS SUDD
Malakāl
Kodok
Nāṣir
Gambela
Jima
Shewa Gimira
Sodo
Wenda
ETHIOPIA
HARERGE
Addis Ababa (Ādīs Ābeba)
Nekemte
Dembi Dolo
Gore
Koundé
Bouar
Fort-Sibut
Bambari
Rafaï
Zémio
Wāw
Shambe
Bor
Pibor
Mongalla
Jūbā
Maji
Bako
Ginir
Goba
Garoua
CENTRAL AFRICAN REPUBLIC
Fort-de-Possel
Bangui
Mbaïki
Zongo
Mobaye
Bangassou
Yalinga
Tambura
Rumbek
Shambe
Kapoeta
SIDAMO
Chew Bahir (Lake Stefanie)
Mega
Moyale
Doolow
ON
Carnot
Bozoum
Mongoumba
Libenge
Mobayi-Mbongo
Bondo
Bambesa
Dungu
Niangara
Arua
Kitgum
Nimule
Lake Rudolf +1230
El Wak
Yokaduma
Lomié
Doumé
Bangui
Businga
Gemena
Aketi
Buta
Isiro
Gombari
Watsa
Mahagi Port
UGANDA
Soroti
KENYA
SOMALIA
Dongou
Ouesso
CONGO
Makanza
Impfondo
Bomongo
Basankusu
Lisala
Bumba
Panga
Avakubi
Irumu
Arua
Masindi
L. Albert
Ft. Portal
Margherita Peak 16 763
Kampala
Jinja
Eldoret
Mt. Elgon 14 178
Meru
Mbandaka
ZAIRE
Kisangani (Stanleyville)
Boyoma Falls
Equator
Entebbe
Lake Victoria

AREA (inset)
40,000 SQ MI AREA
0 100 200 Miles

Scale
0 50 100 200 300 400 500 Miles
0 100 200 400 600 800 Kilometers

Scale 1:16 000 000; one inch to 250 miles. Sinusoidal Projection
Elevations and depressions are given in feet

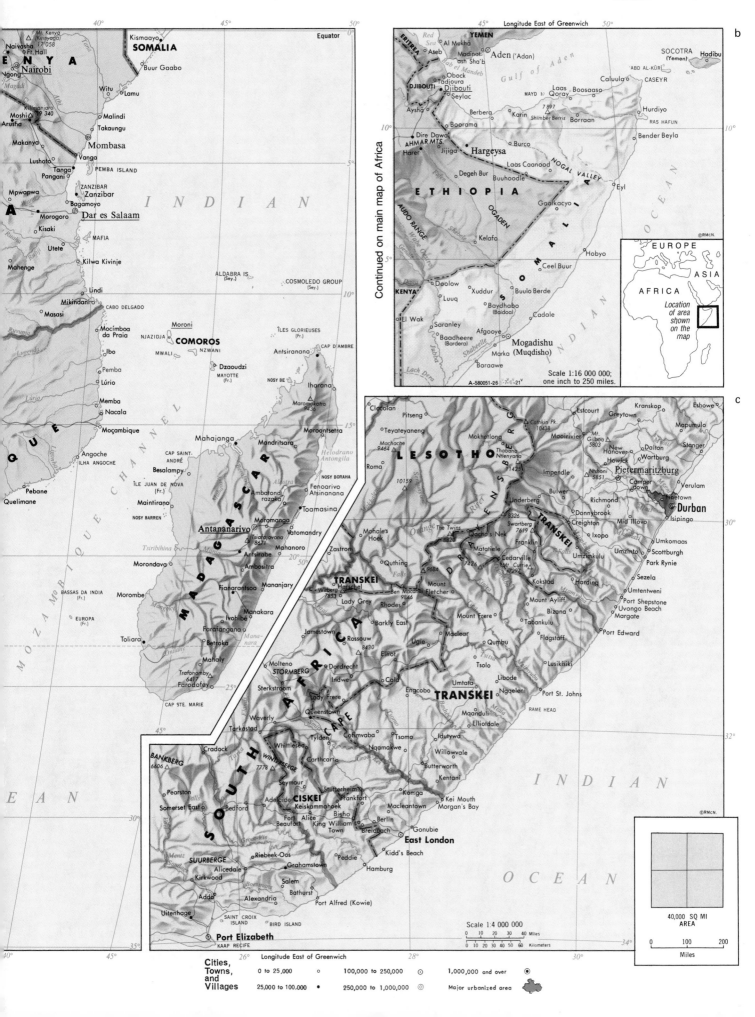

b

KENYA / SOMALIA region (upper left)

Mt. Kenya (Kirinyaga) 17,058
Naivasha Ft. Hall
Ngong
Nairobi
K E N Y A
Magadi
Kilimanjaro 19,340
Moshi Arusha
Makanya
Lushoto
Tanga
Pangani Vanga
Mpwapwa
Morogoro
Kisaki
Utete
Mahenge
Kismaayo
SOMALIA
Buur Gaabo
Witu
Lamu
Malindi
Takaungu
Mombasa
PEMBA ISLAND
ZANZIBAR
Zanzibar
Bagamoyo
Dar es Salaam
MAFIA
Kilwa Kivinje
Lindi
Mikindani CABO DELGADO
Masasi
Ruvuma
Lugenda
Mocímboa da Praia
Ibo
Pemba
Lúrio
Memba
Nacala
Moçambique
Angoche
ILHA ANGOCHE
Pebane
Quelimane

I N D I A N   O C E A N

MOZAMBIQUE CHANNEL

ALDABRA IS. (Sey.)
COSMOLEDO GROUP (Sey.)
ÎLES GLORIEUSES (Fr.)
CAP D'AMBRE
Antsiranana
NOSY BE
Iharana
Maromokotro 9436

Moroni
NJAZIDJA
COMOROS
MWALI NZWANI
Dzaoudzi
MAYOTTE (Fr.)

Mahajanga
Mandritsara
Maroantsetra
Helodrano Antongila
NOSY BORAHA
Besalampy
ÎLE JUAN DE NOVA (Fr.)
NOSY BARREN
Maintirano
Ambatond razaka
Fenoarivo Atsinanana
Moramanga
Toamasina
Antananarivo
Tsiafajavona 8671
Mahanoro
Antsirabe
Mananjary
Ambositra
Morondava
M A D A G A S C A R
Fianarantsoa
Manakara
BASSAS DA INDIA (Fr.)
Ivohibé
EUROPA (Fr.)
Farafangana
Morombe
Betroka
Mahaly
Trafonomby 6417
Farodofay
Toliara
CAP STE. MARIE

Somalia inset (b)

Continued on main map of Africa

Longitude East of Greenwich

ERITREA
Red Sea
Al Mukha
YEMEN
Madinat ash Sha'b
Aden ('Adan)
Bab el Mandeb
Gulf of Aden
SOCOTRA (Yemen)
Hadibu
ABD AL-KÜRI
Aseb
DJIBOUTI
Tadjoura
Djibouti
Obock
Seylac
MAYD Is
Laas Qoray
Boosaaso
Caluula
CASEYR
Aysha
Berbera
Karin
Hurdiyo
RAS HAFUN
Boorama
7897
Shimber Berris
Borraan
Bender Beyla
AHMAR MTS.
Dire Dawa
Harer
Jijiga
Hargeysa
Laas Caanood
NOGAL VALLEY
Burco
Degeh Bur
Buuhoodle
Eyl
ETHIOPIA
AUDO RANGE
Gaalkacyo
Shebele
Kelafa
Wabe Gestro
S O M A L I A
Ceel Buur
Hobyo
Genale
Doolow
KENYA
Xuddur
Buulo Berde
Luuq
Baydhabo (Baidoa)
Cadale
El Wak
Saranley
Afgooye
Baadheere (Bardera)
Mogadishu (Muqdisho)
Juba
Shabeelle
Marka
Lach Dera
Baraawe

EUROPE
ASIA
AFRICA
Location of area shown on the map

Scale 1:16 000 000;
one inch to 250 miles.

A-580051-26

c

South Africa / Lesotho / Transkei region (c)

Clocolan
Pitseng
Estcourt
Kranskop
Eshowe
Teyateyaneng
Cathkin Pk. 10438
Greytown
Mapumulo
Mokhotlong
Mooirivier
Mt. Gilboa 5803
New Hanover
Dalton
Stanger
Machache 9464
Thabana Ntlenyana 11425
L E S O T H O
Roma
Impendle
Howick
Ntshoni 5851
Wartburg
Pietermaritzburg
10159
Bulwer
Richmond
Camperdown
Verulam
Pinetown
Durban
Underberg
Mohale's Hoek
Orange
The Twins
Qacha's Nek
9326
Swartberg 7619
Donnybrook
Creighton
Mid Illovo
Isipingo
Zastron
Matatiele
Franklin
T R A N S K E I
Ixopo
Umkomaas
Quthing
9684
Cedarville 7426
Mt. Currie 7297
Kokstad
Umzinkulu
Scottburgh
Park Rynie
Herschel
Wilberg 7853
Ben Macdhui 9846
Mount Fletcher
Harding
Sezela
Lady Grey
Rhodes
Mount
Bizana
Umtentweni
Jamestown
Barkly East
Mount Frere
Mount Aylff
Tabankulu
Port Shepstone
Rossouw 8430
Ugie
Maclear
Flagstaff
Uvongo Beach
Margate
Elliot
Qumbu
Tsolo
Lusikisiki
Port Edward
Molteno
Dordrecht
Indwe
Cala
Engcobo
Umtata
Libode
Ngqeleni
Port St. Johns
Sterkstroom
STORMBERG
Lady Frere
T R A N S K E I
RAME HEAD
Waverly
Queenstown
Tylden
Cofimvaba
Tsomo
Mqanduli
Elliotdale
Tarkastad
Cradock
Whittlesea
Carthcarto
Ngamakwe
Willowvale
Cathcart
Ngqamakwe
BANKBERG 6606
WINTERBERG 7778
Seymour
Stutterheim
Butterworth
Kentani
Pearston
Frankfort
Komga
Kei Mouth
Adelaide
C I S K E I
Macleantown
Morgan's Bay
Somerset East
Keiskammahoek
Bisho
Berlin
Bedford
Fort Alice
King William's Town
Breidbach
Gonubie
Beaufort
East London
Riebeek-Oos
Peddie
Kidd's Beach
SUURBERGE
Alicedale
Grahamstown
Hamburg
Kirkwood
Salem
Addo
Bathurst
Alexandria
Port Alfred (Kowie)
Uitenhage
SAINT CROIX ISLAND
BIRD ISLAND
Port Elizabeth
KAAP RECIFE

S O U T H   A F R I C A
C A P E
DRAKENSBERG
Umkomaas

I N D I A N   O C E A N

Scale 1:4 000 000
0 10 20 30 40 Miles
0 10 20 30 40 50 60 Kilometers

40,000 SQ MI
AREA
0   100   200
Miles

©RMcN.

Longitude East of Greenwich

Cities, Towns, and Villages
0 to 25,000   100,000 to 250,000   1,000,000 and over
25,000 to 100,000   250,000 to 1,000,000   Major urbanized area

Cities,
Towns,
and
Villages

0 to 25,000 ○   100,000 to 250,000 ⊙   1,000,000 and over ◉

25,000 to 100,000 ●   250,000 to 1,000,000 ◎   Major urbanized area

Scale 1: 12 000 000; one inch to 190 miles. Conic Projection

Elevations and depressions are given in feet

Longitude West of Greenwich

Longitude West of Greenwich

Same scale as main map

QUEBEC

CAPE BAULD

Gulf of St. Lawrence

Strait of Belle Isle

C. ST. JOHN

LONG RANGE MTS.

White Bay

Notre Dame Bay

Twillingate

GROS MORNE NAT'L PARK
Deer Lake
Corner Brook
Stephenville
C. ST. GEORGE

Grand Falls
Botwood
Windsor
Gander

Bonavista Bay
Bonavista

TERRA NOVA NAT'L PARK

St. George's Bay

St. George's

NEWFOUNDLAND

Trinity
Trinity Bay

Cabot Strait

CAPE RAY
CAPE NORTH

Channel-Port-aux-Basques

St. Pierre and Miquelon (Fr.)

Grand Bank
Fortune Bay
Burin

Placentia Bay

St. John's

CAPE BRETON ISLAND

ATLANTIC OCEAN

©RMcN

BAFFIN ISLAND

BAFFIN ISLAND NAT'L PARK
Pangnirtung
CUMBERLAND PEN.
Netilling
Cumberland Sound

PRINCE CHARLES ISLAND

MERCY

ES

Gulf of Boothia

MELVILLE PENINSULA

Igloolik

Foxe Basin

Arctic Circle

HALL PEN.

C. DYER

Frobisher Bay

Iqaluit

EVERETT MTS.

Lake Harbour

RESOLUTION

SALISBURY

Hudson

SOUTHAMPTON ISLAND

C. LOW

COATS

MANSEL

NOTTINGHAM ISLAND

BELL PEN.

Fisher Strait

Roes Welcome Sound

Wager Bay

Foxe Channel

KILLINIQ I.

C. HOPES ADVANCE

AKPATOK

C. DE NOUVELLE-FRANCE

Strait

Ivujivik

PENINSULE D'UNGAVA

Payne

Ungava Bay

TORNGAT MTS.

Hebron

Nain

Hopedale

HUDSON BAY

All islands within bays and straits
lie within Northwest Territories.

Povungnituk

OTTAWA ISLANDS

aux Feuilles

Kuujjuaq

Koksoak

Makkovik

Rigolet

Hamilton Inlet

Cartwright

NEW

MEALY MTS.

Happy Valley
Goose Bay

Vaikaupi

FOU

Michikamau

Battle Harbour

Minto

Lac Bienville

Caniapiscau

LABRADOR

St. Anthony

BELCHER ISLANDS

Grande de la Baleine

Schefferville

Churchill Falls

Little Mecatina

LONG RANGE MTS.

GROS MORNE NAT'L PARK

Corner Brook
Stephenville
St. George

C. HENRIETTA MARIA

PTE. LOUIS-XIV

La Grande

Nichicun

Lac Ashuanipi

R. aux Outardes

Romaine

Natashquan

Ft. Severn

James Bay

Chisasibi

AKIMISKI

Easmain

Opinaca

Nottaway

MTS. OTISH

Lac Manicouagan

ILE D'ANTICOSTI

Mingan

Natashquan

Winisk

Severn

Ft. Albany

Moosonee

Mistassini

Chibougamau

Peribonca

Mistassibi

St. Lawrence River

Cap Chat

MTS. CHIC-CHOCS

Gaspé

PEN. DE GASPE

New Carlisle
Chandler

ILES DE LA MADELEINE

PRINCE EDWARD NAT'L PARK

New Waterford

Q U E B E C

O N T A R I O

St. Joseph

St. Felicien

Roberval
Chambord

Dolbeau
Alma
Kenogami

Arvida

Lac St. Jean

Jonquière Chicoutimi

Saguenay

Betsiamites

Rimouski

Riviere-du-Loup

Mont-Joli

Matane

Campbellton

Bathurst

NEW BRUNSWICK

Newcastle
Chatham
Richibucto

Summerside

P.E.I.

Charlottetown

Amherst

New Glasgow
Pictou
Stellarton
Antigonish
New Glasgow

Sydney Mines
North Sydney
Sydney

Trout Lake

Red Lake

Lac Seul

Sioux Lookout

Kenora

Dryden

English

Lake of the Woods

Rainy

Ft. Frances

Rainy River

Thunder Bay

St. Joseph

Armstrong Sta.

Geraldton
Longlac

Nakina

Hearst

Kapuskasing

Cochrane
Iroquois Falls

Timmins

Oba

Kirkland Lake

Cobalt

Ville Marie

Temiscaming

Abitibi

La Sarre

Amos
Senneterre

Rouyn
Malartic Val-d'Or

Reservoir Gouin

Parent

La Tuque

St. Maurice

Shawinigan
Grand Mere

Trois-Rivieres

Joliette

Matagami

Waswanipi

Chapleau

Marathon

PUKASKWA NAT'L PARK

MICHIPICOTEN

Nipigon

Nipigon

Lake Superior

Thessalon

Blind River

Espanola

Sudbury

Sturgeon Falls

North Bay

Mattawa

Pembroke

Renfrew

Ottawa

Hull

MONTRÉAL

St. Jerome

Valleyfield

St. Jean

St. Hyacinthe

Drummondville

Sorel

Sherbrooke

Granby

Québec

Lévis

a la Malbaie
Baie St. Paul

Montmagny

Victoriaville

CANADA U.S.A.

St. Frontiere

MAINE

Woodstock

Fredericton

Edmundston

Grand Falls

Moncton

Sussex

Saint John

St. Andrews
St. Stephen

St. George

FUNDY NAT'L PARK

Bay of Fundy

Digby

Kentville

Windsor

Truro

Dartmouth
Halifax

NOVA SCOTIA

Lunenburg
Bridgewater
Liverpool

Shelburne

Yarmouth

CAPE SABLE

MICHIGAN

Sault Ste. Marie

Sault Ste. Marie

Marquette

Escanaba

Duluth

Superior

MANITOULIN

Georgian Bay

Little Current

Parry Sound

Huntsville

Bracebridge

Smiths Falls

Brockville

Ogdensburg

Alexandria Bay

Kingston

NEW YORK

Watertown

VERMONT

NEW HAMPSHIRE

Montpelier

Concord

Augusta

Portland

MASS.

Harvard

Boston

CAPE COD

Thunder Bay

MINNESOTA

WISCONSIN

St. Paul

MINNEAPOLIS

Madison

Green Bay

MILWAUKEE

CHICAGO

ILL.

Saginaw

Flint

Grand Rapids

Lansing

DETROIT

Leamington

Windsor

Sarnia
Chatham

Port Huron

London

St. Thomas

Wiarton

Owen Sound

Kincardine

Midland

Barrie

Orillia

Collingwood

Simcoe

TORONTO

Oshawa

Whitby

Kitchener

Hamilton

St. Catharines

Niagara Falls

BUFFALO

Rochester

Lake Ontario

Peterborough

Cobourg

Trenton

Belleville

Lake Erie

Toledo

OHIO

PENNSYLVANIA

Scranton

Albany

NEW YORK

N.J.

CONN.

Providence

R.I.

Hartford

ATLANTIC OCEAN

Cornwall

40,000 SQ MI
AREA

0   100   200

Miles

0   25 50 75 100   200   300   400   500 Miles

0   100   200   400   600   800 Kilometers

A-520200-26—9-8-18V
COPYRIGHT BY
RAND McNALLY & COMPANY
MADE IN U.S.A.

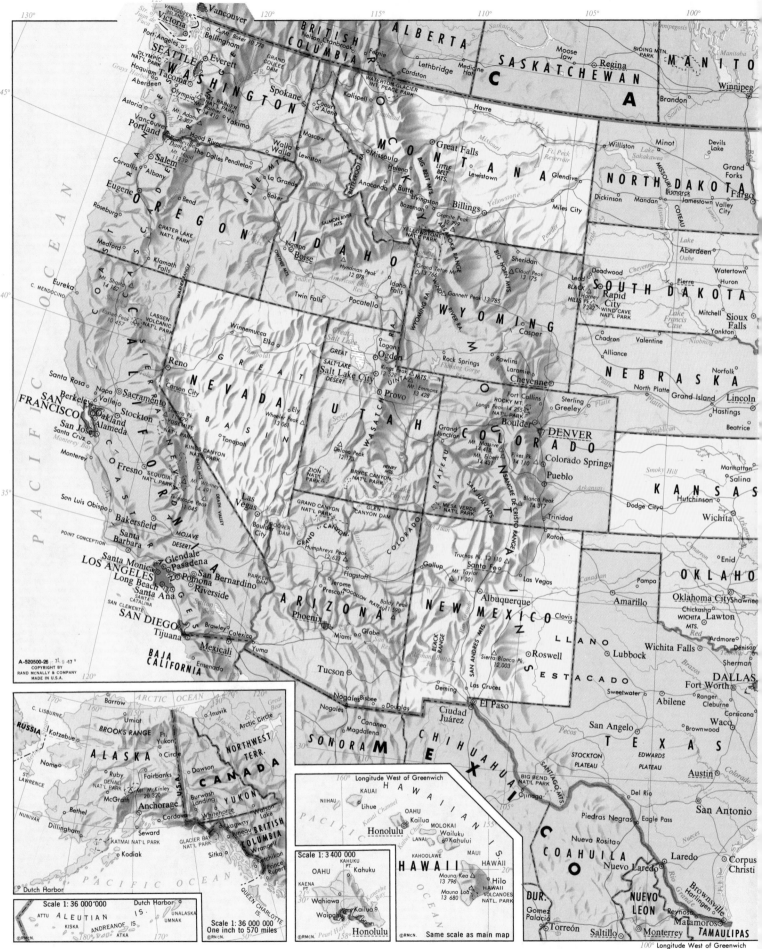

Scale 1:12 000 000; one inch to 190 miles. Polyconic Projection
Elevations and depressions are given in feet

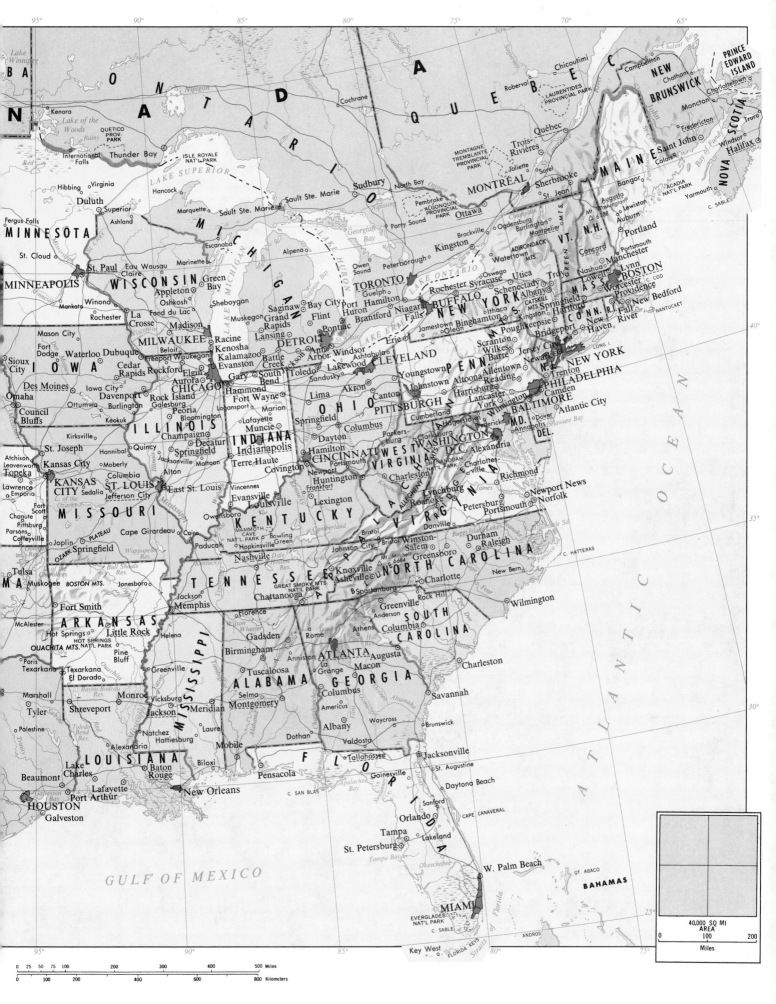

Scale 1:4 000 000; one inch to 64 miles. Conic Projection
Elevations and depressions are given in feet

Longitude West of Greenwich

2,500 SQ MI
AREA

0   50
Miles

Scale 1:4 000 000; one inch to 64 miles. Conic Projection
Elevations and depressions are given in feet

Longitude West of Greenwich

A-51100526 -98-13
COPYRIGHT BY
RAND McNALLY & COMPANY
MADE IN U.S.A.

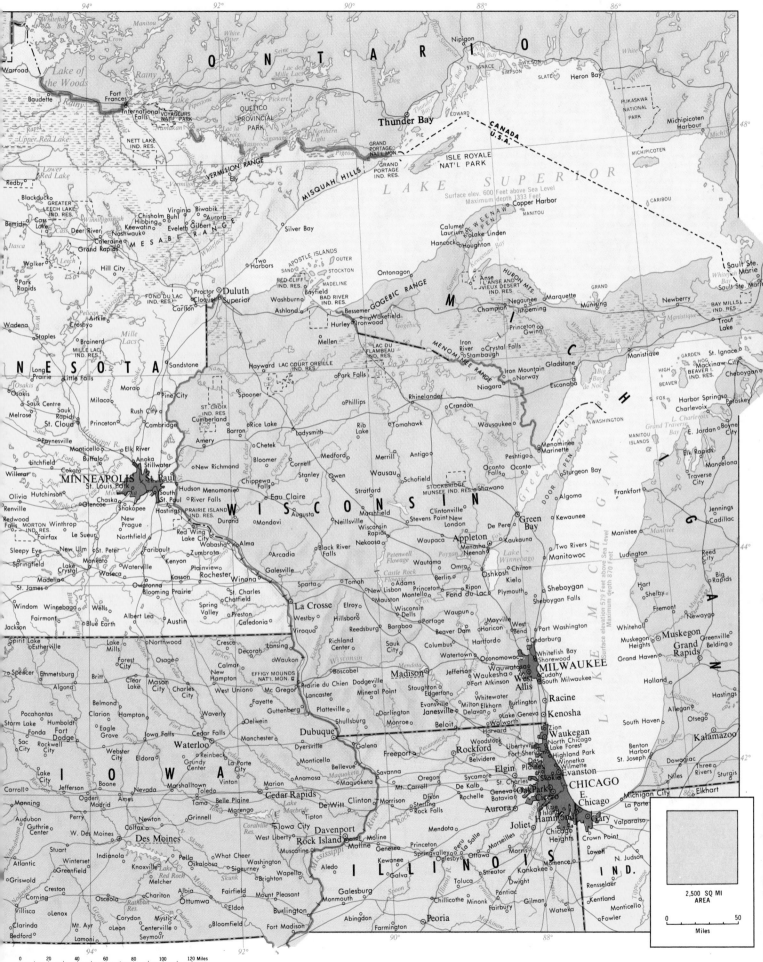

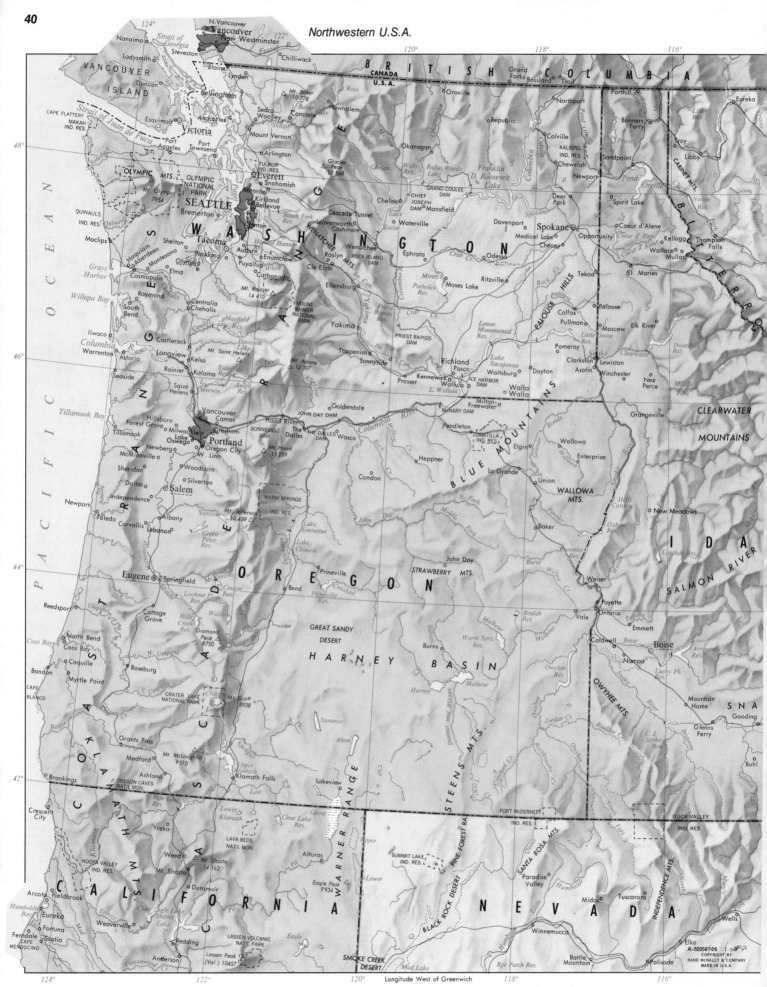

Scale 1: 4 000 000; one inch to 64 miles. Conic Projection
Elevations and depressions are given in feet

Longitude West of Greenwich

2,500 SQ MI
AREA

0   50
Miles

Scale 1:4 000 000; one inch to 64 miles. Conic Projection
Elevations and depressions are given in feet

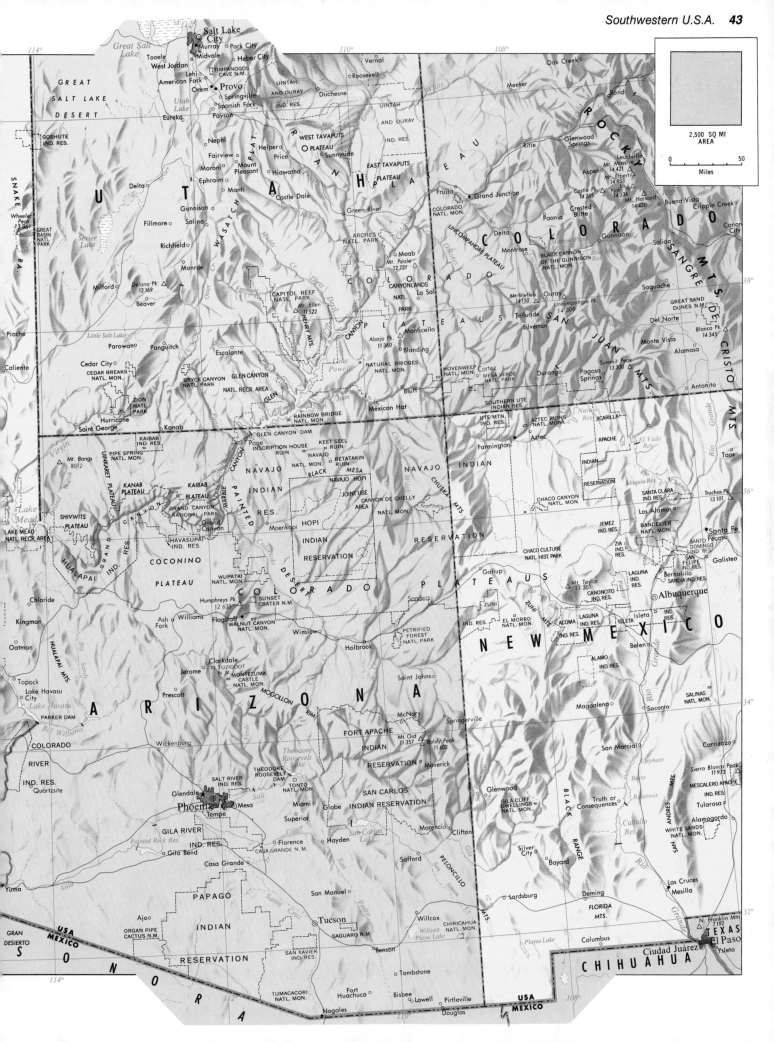

2,500 SQ MI
AREA

0   50
Miles

Salt Lake City
Tooele
Murray
Midvale
Park City
Heber City
West Jordan
American Fork
Lehi
Orem
Provo
Springville
Spanish Fork
Payson
Eureka
Delta
Nephi
Fairview
Moroni
Mount Pleasant
Ephraim
Manti
Gunnison
Salina
Fillmore
Castle Dale
Richfield
Monroe
Milford
Beaver
Parowan
Panguitch
Escalante
Cedar City
Hurricane
Saint George
Kanab

GREAT SALT LAKE DESERT
GOSHUTE IND. RES.
SNAKE RA.
Wheeler Peak 13 061
GREAT BASIN NATL. PARK
Pioche
Caliente
Sevier Lake
Little Salt Lake
Delano Pk. 12 169

Vernal
Roosevelt
Duchesne
Oak Creek
Meeker
Bond
Rifle
Glenwood Springs
Leadville
Aspen Mt. Massive 14 421
Mt. Elbert 14 433
Castle Pk. 14 265
Mt. Harvard 14 420
Buena Vista
Cripple Creek
Paonia
Crested Butte
Canon City
Gunnison
Salida
Saguache
Del Norte
Monte Vista
Alamosa
Antonito

UINTAH AND OURAY IND. RES.
WEST TAVAPUTS PLATEAU
EAST TAVAPUTS PLATEAU
Helper
Price
Sunnyside
Hiawatha
Castle Dale
Green River
Fruita
Grand Junction
COLORADO NATL. MON.
UNCOMPAHGRE PLATEAU
Delta
Montrose

UTAH
COLORADO

WASATCH PLAT.
Utah Lake

ARCHES NATL. PARK
Moab
Mt. Peale 12 721
CANYONLANDS NATL. PARK
La Sal
Mt. Sneffels 14 150
Uncompahgre Pk. 14 309
Ouray
Telluride
Silverton
GREAT SAND DUNES N.M.
Blanca Pk. 14 345

CAPITOL REEF NATL. PARK
Mt. Ellen 11 522
HENRY MTS.
Abajo Pk. 11 360
Monticello
Blanding
NATURAL BRIDGES NATL. MON.
HOVENWEEP NATL. MON.
Cortez
MESA VERDE NATL. PARK
Durango
Pagosa Springs
Summit Peak 13 300
SAN JUAN MTS.
SANGRE DE CRISTO MTS.

BRYCE CANYON NATL. PARK
CEDAR BREAKS NATL. MON.
ZION NATL. PARK
GLEN CANYON NATL. RECR. AREA
Lake Powell
Bluff
Mexican Hat
RAINBOW BRIDGE NATL. MON.
GLEN CANYON DAM
Page
INSCRIPTION HOUSE RUIN
KEET SEEL RUIN
BETATAKIN RUIN
NAVAJO NATL. MON.
SOUTHERN UTE IND. RES.
UTE MTN. IND. RES.
AZTEC RUINS NATL. MON.
Navajo Res.
JICARILLA
APACHE
El Vado Res.
Taos

KAIBAB IND. RES.
PIPE SPRING NATL. MON.
Mt. Bangs 8012
KANAB PLATEAU
KAIBAB PLATEAU
MARBLE CANYON
PAINTED
NAVAJO INDIAN RES.
BLACK MESA
NAVAJO HOPI JOINT USE AREA
CANYON DE CHELLY NATL. MON.
CHUSKA MTS.
NAVAJO INDIAN RESERVATION
Farmington
Aztec
INDIAN RESERVATION
CHACO CANYON NATL. MON.
Abiquiu Res.
SANTA CLARA IND. RES.
Truchas Pk. 13 101

UINKARET PLATEAU
SHIVWITS PLATEAU
HUALAPAI IND. RES.
LAKE MEAD NATL. RECR. AREA
Lake Mead
Chloride
Kingman
Oatman
Topock
Lake Havasu City
PARKER DAM
Bill Williams
Big Sandy
COLORADO RIVER IND. RES.
Quartzsite

GRAND CANYON NATIONAL PARK
Grand Canyon
HAVASUPAI IND. RES.
Moenkopi
HOPI INDIAN RESERVATION
COCONINO PLATEAU
WUPATKI NATL. MON.
Humphreys Pk. 12 633
SUNSET CRATER N.M.
Ash Fork
Williams
Flagstaff
WALNUT CANYON NATL. MON.
Winslow
Holbrook
COLORADO DESERT
Little Colorado
Sanders
PETRIFIED FOREST NATL. PARK

CHACO CULTURE NATL. HIST. PARK
Gallup
Mt. Taylor 11 301
JEMEZ IND. RES.
BANDELIER NATL. MON.
Los Alamos
Santa Fe
SANTO DOMINGO IND. RES.
SAN FELIPE IND. RES.
Galisteo
ZIA IND. RES.
CANONCITO IND. RES.
LAGUNA IND. RES.
SANDIA IND. RES.
Bernalillo
Albuquerque

ZUNI
ZUNI MTS.
EL MORRO NATL. MON.
ACOMA IND. RES.
LAGUNA IND. RES.
Isleta
ISLETA IND. RES.
Belen

ARIZONA
NEW MEXICO

Clarkdale
TUZIGOOT N.M.
Jerome
MONTEZUMA CASTLE NATL. MON.
Prescott
MOGOLLON RIM
Saint Johns
McNary
Springerville
Mt. Ord 11 357
Baldy Peak 11 403
Maverick
FORT APACHE INDIAN RESERVATION
Theodore Roosevelt Lake
THEODORE ROOSEVELT DAM
TONTO NATL. MON.
Glendale
SALT RIVER IND. RES.
Phoenix
Tempe
Mesa
Salt
Miami
Globe
SAN CARLOS INDIAN RESERVATION
San Carlos Lake
Superior
Florence
CASA GRANDE N.M.
Hayden
Morenci
Clifton
Safford
PELONCILLO MTS.

San Marcial
Magdalena
Socorro
ALAMO IND. RES.
Carrizozo
Sierra Blanca Peak 11 973
MESCALERO APACHE IND. RES.
Tularosa
Alamogordo
WHITE SANDS NATL. MON.
SALINAS NATL. MON.
Elephant Butte
Glenwood
GILA CLIFF DWELLINGS NATL. MON.
Truth or Consequences
Caballo Res.
BLACK RANGE
SAN ANDRES MTS.
SAN MATEO MTS.

GILA RIVER IND. RES.
Gila Bend
PAPAGO INDIAN RESERVATION
Ajo
ORGAN PIPE CACTUS N.M.
Painted Rock Res.
Casa Grande
Florence
San Manuel
San Xavier IND. RES.
SAN XAVIER IND. RES.
Silver City
Bayard
Lordsburg
Deming
FLORIDA MTS.
Las Cruces
Mesilla

Yuma
GRAN DESIERTO
SONORA
USA MEXICO
TUMACACORI NATL. MON.
Nogales
Fort Huachuca
Bisbee
Lowell
Pirtleville
Douglas
Tombstone
Benson
Tucson
SAGUARO N.M.
Willcox
CHIRICAHUA NATL. MON.
Willcox Playa Lake
Playas Lake
Columbus
USA MEXICO
CHIHUAHUA
Ciudad Juárez
TEXAS
El Paso
Ysleta
N. Franklin Mtn. 7192

2,500 SQ MI
AREA

0   50
Miles

A-511006-26   7-7-10
COPYRIGHT BY
RAND McNALLY & COMPANY
MADE IN U.S.A.

Longitude West of Greenwich

Scale 1:4 000 000; one inch to 64 miles. Conic Projection
Elevations and depressions are given in feet.

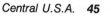

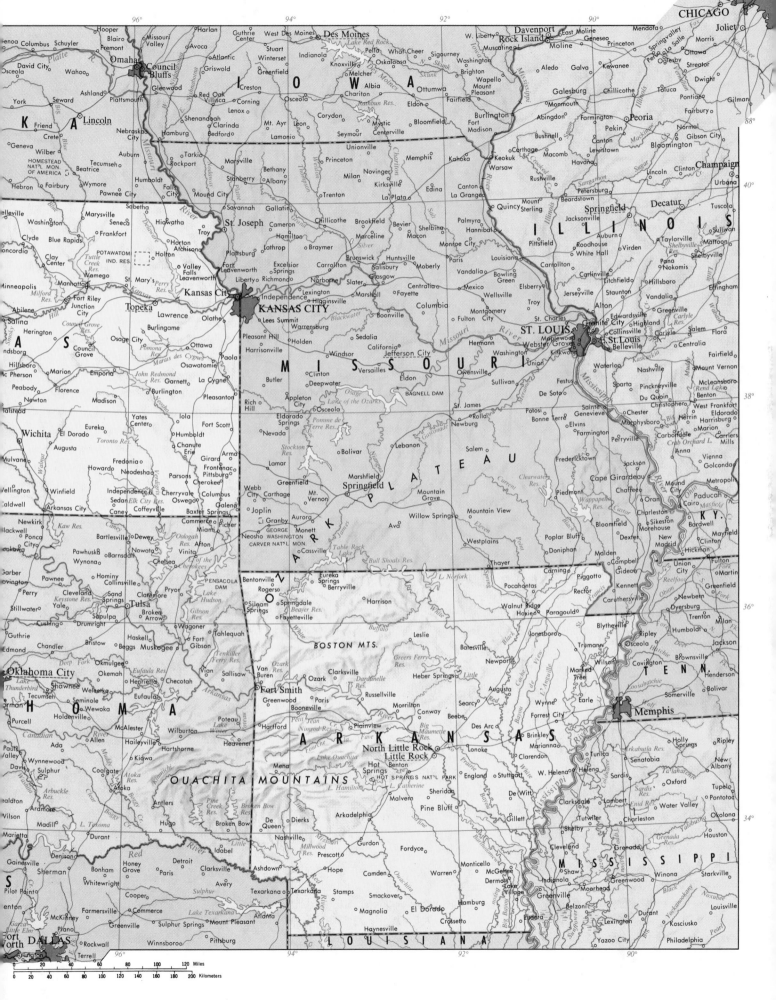

NEW MEXICO

Alamogordo
△ Alamo Pk.
7820
WHITE SANDS
NAT'L MON.
N. Franklin Mtn.
7176
El Paso
Ysleta
Ciudad Juárez
Fabens
Guadalupe
Villa
Ahumada

Artesia
Dayton
McMillan
Hobbs
Carlsbad
CARLSBAD
CAVERNS
NAT'L PARK
Wind Mtn.
7278
Red Bluff Res.
Guadalupe Pk.
8751
Pecos
Toyah

Seagraves
Seminole
O'Donnell
Lamesa
Snyder
Big Spring
Midland
Stanton
Wink
Odessa
Sterling City

Haskell
Hamlin
Stamford
Rotan
Roscoe
Sweetwater
Merkel
Baird
Colorado
City

Newcastle
Graham
Mineral Wells
Breckenridge
Anson
Albany
Abilene
Ranger
Strawn
Thurber
Eastland
Cisco
Desdemona
Gorman
De Leon
Stephenville
Dublin
Hico

GUADALUPE MTS.

Sierra Blanca
Van Horn
Eagle Pk.
7496

DAVIS MTS.
Baldy Peak
8382
Marfa
Alpine

Fort Stockton
McCamey
Sanderson

STOCKTON
PLATEAU

Sterling City
San Angelo
Eden
Brady
Menard
Sonora
Junction

Winters
Ballinger
Coleman
Santa Anna
Brownwood
Goldthwaite

Comanche
Hamilton
San Saba
Lometa
Lampasas
Burnet

T E X A S

E D W A R D S   P L A T E A U

Rocksprings
Fredericksburg
Kerrville

Camp Wood

Llano
Mason
Llano

San
Marcos
Boerne
New Braunfels
Seguin
San Antonio
Hondo

SANTIAGO MTS.
Cathedral Pk
6860
Chinati Pk.
7730
Presidio
Ojinaga
Coyame
Cuchillo Parado

BIG BEND
NAT'L PARK
△ Emory Pk.
7835

Aldama

Chihuahua

C H I H U A H U A

Meogui
Naica

U.S.A.
MEXICO
SERRANÍAS
DEL BURRO
Del Rio
Villa Acuña
Brackettville
Jiménez

Piedras Negras
Fuente
Eagle Pass
Zaragoza
Morelos
Nava
Allende
Guerrero
Rosales

Muzquiz
San Juan de Sabinas

Uvalde
Sabinal

Crystal City
Carrizo Springs
Asherton

Floresville
Poteet
Pleasanton
Pearsall

Cotulla
Fowlerton

Kenedy

George
West
Encinal

San Diego
Corpus Christi
Alice

S I E R R A

M A D R E

S A N   P E D R O

Ciudad Camargo
(Santa Rosalia)
Jaco

C O A H U I L A

BOLSÓN
Sierra Mojada
Laguna de
la Leche

Progreso
Abasolo
Sacramento
San Buenaventura
Nadadores
Monclova

Presa de
D. Martin
Hidalgo
Dolores
Nuevo Laredo
Laredo
Mirando City
Hebbronville
Premont
Falfurrias
Zapata
Guerrero
Falcon Res.

O R I E N T A L

D E
Jimenez
Valle de Allende
Escalon
Villa Lopez
Villa Coronado

Hidalgo
del Parral
Santa Barbara
Rosario
Villa
Ocampo

M E X

Indé

MAPIMI

Sierra Mojada

Cuatro Ciénegas

Lampazos
Bustamante
Villaldama
Sabinas Hidalgo
Aqualeguas
Mier
Camargo
Riogrande
Mission
Edinburg
McAllen
Weslaco
Reynosa
Matamoros

N U E V O

Paredon
Garcia
Salinas Victoria
General Zuazua
Cerralvo
Los Herreras

Presa
Azucar

I C O

Santa Cruz

Mapimi
Sacramento
San Pedro
de las Colonias
Laguna
de
Mayran
Gómez Palacio
Lerdo
Torreón
Matamoros
Laguna de
Viesca
Parras
Viesca

San Luis del
Cordero
Rodeo
Nazas

D U R A N G O

San Juan del Rio
Cuencame
Pánuco de
Coronado

Canatlán

Durango

Ramos Arizpe
General Cepeda
Arteaga
Saltillo

Monterrey
Santa Catarina

Gomez Farias

Galeana
Linares

L E O N

Villa de Allende
Montemorelos

China
Cadereyta Jimenez

T A M A U L I P A S

San Bartolo
San Juan de
Guadalupe

Mazapil
Concepción
del Oro

Z A C A T E C A S

Santa Clara
Juan Aldama

Burgos
San
Fernando
Cruillas
San Carlos
Villagran

2,500 SQ MI
AREA
0   50
Miles

Scale 1:4 000 000; one inch to 64 miles. Conic Projection
Elevations and depressions are given in feet

Scale 1:1 000 000

0   5   10 Miles
0 4 8 12 16 Kilometers

®RMCN

0 20 40 60 80 100 120 Miles
0 20 40 60 80 100 120 140 160 180 200 Kilometers

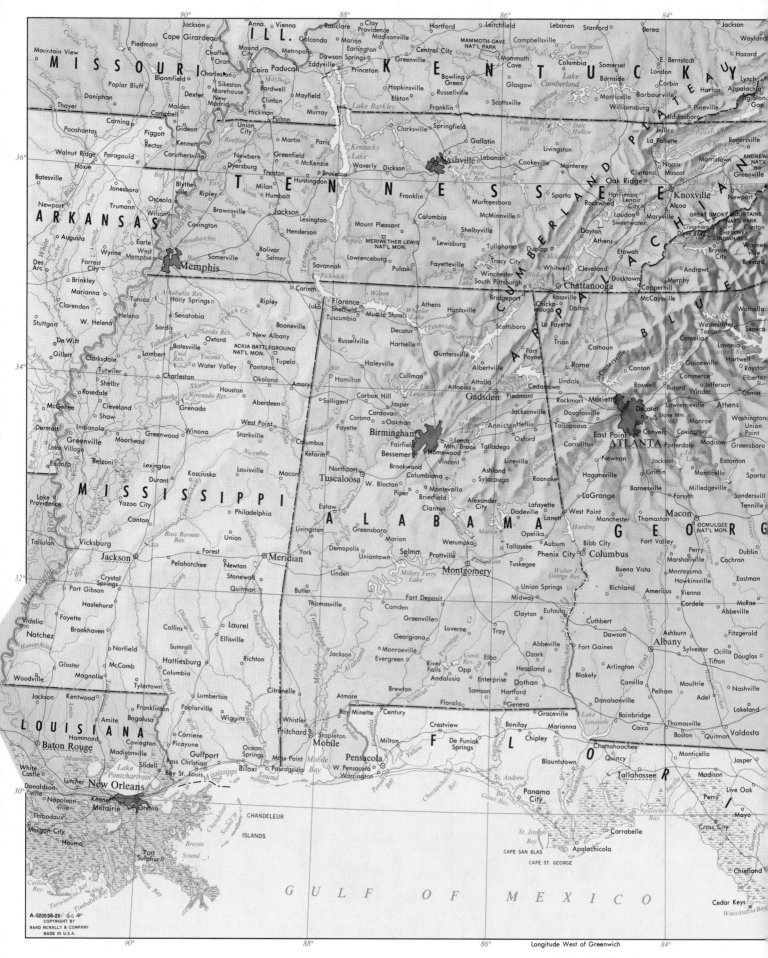

A-520598-26- 6-6 -9V
COPYRIGHT BY
RAND McNALLY & COMPANY
MADE IN U.S.A.

Longitude West of Greenwich

Scale 1:4 000 000; one inch to 64 miles. Conic Projection
Elevations and depressions are given in feet

2,500 SQ MI
AREA

0   50
Miles

A-530000-26- -9-6-24'
COPYRIGHT BY
RAND McNALLY & COMPANY
MADE IN U.S.A.

Scale 1:16 000 000; one inch to 250 miles. Polyconic Projection
Elevations and depressions are given in feet

a

PANAMA

Scale 1:1 000 000

0   5   10 Miles
0 4 8 12 16 Kilometers

DAVID C. WEST

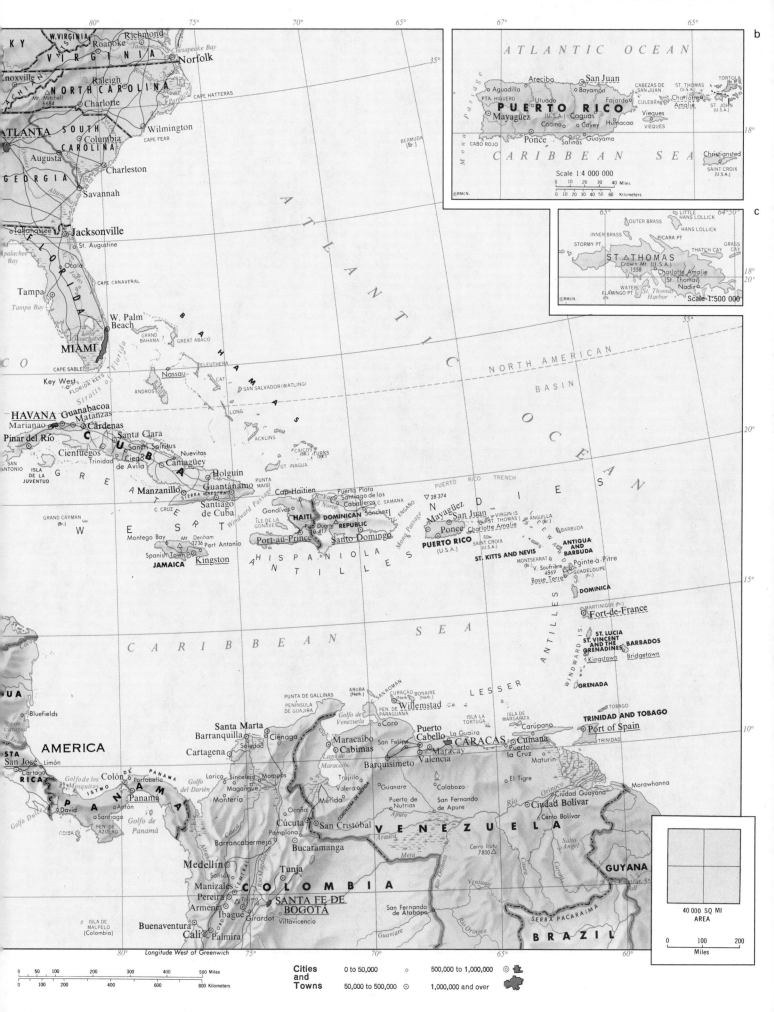

Scale 1:4 000 000

0 10 20 30 40 Miles
0 10 20 30 40 50 60 Kilometers

Scale 1:500 000

Cities
and
Towns

0 to 50,000	○ 500,000 to 1,000,000
50,000 to 500,000	⊙ 1,000,000 and over

40 000 SQ MI
AREA

0 100 200
Miles

0 50 100 200 300 400 500 Miles
0 100 200 400 600 800 Kilometers

Longitude West of Greenwich

52

CARIBBEAN SEA

PACIFIC OCEAN

NICARAGUA
COSTA RICA
PANAMA
COLOMBIA
ECUADOR
PERU
VENEZUELA
BOLIVIA
ARGENTINA

ARCHIPIELAGO DE COLON (GALÁPAGOS ISLANDS) (Ecuador)

AMAZO SELVAS

Equator

Tropic of Capricorn

A-549100-26   9-10-49
COPYRIGHT BY
RAND McNALLY & COMPANY
MADE IN U.S.A.

Scale 1:16 000 000: one inch to 250 miles. Sinusoidal Projection
Elevations and depressions are given in feet

Longitude West

Scale 1:4 000 000
0   10   20   30   40 Miles
0 10 20 30 40 50 60 Kilometers

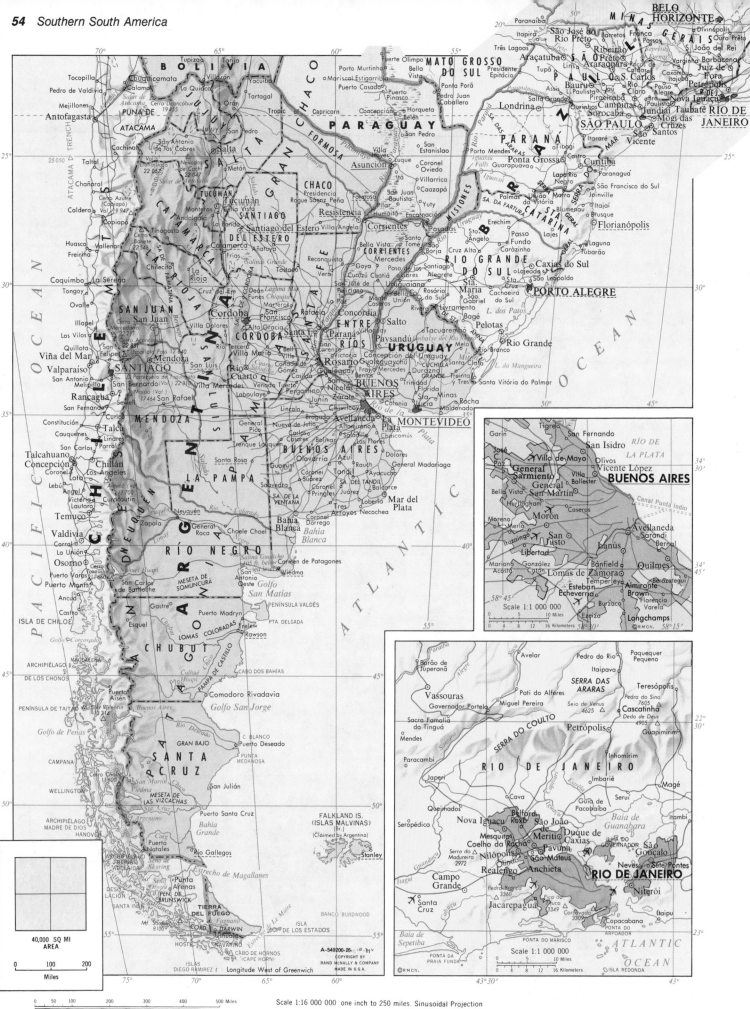

Scale 1:16 000 000 one inch to 250 miles. Sinusoidal Projection
Elevations and depressions are given in feet

BUENOS AIRES

Scale 1:1 000 000

RIO DE JANEIRO

Scale 1:1 000 000

40,000 SQ MI AREA

Index

ABBREVIATIONS OF GEOGRAPHICAL NAMES AND TERMS

A

13 Aachen, Ger. . . . . .51N 6 E
22 Ābādān, Iran . . . . .30N 48 E
17 Abakan, Russia . . . . .54N 91 E
16 Abdulino, Russia . . . . . .54N 54 E
28 Abeokuta, Nig. . . . . .7N 3 E
12 Aberdeen, Scot. . . . . . . .57N 2 W
38 Aberdeen, S. Dak. 45N 98W
40 Aberdeen, Wash. 47N 124W
28 Abidjan, C. Iv. . . . . .5N 4 W
46 Abilene, Tex. 32N 100W
28 Abuja, Nig. . . . . .9N 7 E
22 Abū Kamāl, Syr. . . . . . . .34N 41 E
22 Abū Zaby, U.A.E. . . . . . .24N 54 E
50 Acapulco, Mex. 17N 100W
28 Accra, Ghana 6N 0
54 Aconcagua, C. (Mt.) Arg. 33S 70W
15 Acre, Isr. . . . . .33N 35 E
15 Adana, Tur. . . . . .37N 35 E
15 Adapazari, Tur. . . . . . . .41N 30 E
22 Ad Dawhah, Qatar . . . . .25N 51 E
22 Ad Dilam, Sau. Ar. . . . . .24N 47 E
22 Addis Ababa, Eth. . . . . . . .9N 39 E
26 Adelaide, Austl. . . . . . . .35S 139 E
22 Aden, Yemen . . . . .13N 45 E
22 Aden, Gulf of, Asia-Afr. . 12N 46 E
37 Adirondack Mts., N.Y. . . .44N 74W
14 Adriatic Sea, Eur. . . . . . .44N 14 E
15 Aegean Sea, Grc.-Tur. . . .39N 25 E
22 Afghanistan (Ctry.) Asia . .34N 65 E
31 Afgooye, Som. . . . . .2N 45 E
14 Aflou, Alg. . . . . .34N 2 E
15 Afyon, Tur. . . . . .39N 30 E
28 Agadir, Mor. 30N 10W
17 Aginskoye, Russia . . . . . .51N 114 E
23 Āgra, India . . . . .27N 78 E
15 Agrínion, Grc. . . . . .39N 21 E
50 Aguascalientes, Mex. 22N 102W
30 Agulhas, C., S. Afr. . . . . .35S 20 E
28 Ahaggar (Mts.) Alg. . . . . .23N 6 E
23 Ahmadābād, India . . . . . .23N 73 E
23 Ahmadnagar, India . . . . .19N 75 E
22 Ahvāz, Iran . . . . .31N 49 E
14 Aïn-Temouchent, Alg. . . .35N 1 W
25 Aitape, Pap. N. Gui. . . . . .3S 142 E
13 Aix-en-Provence, Fr. . . . .44N 5 E
13 Ajaccio, Fr. . . . . .42N 9 E
22 Ajman, U.A.E. . . . . .25N 55 E
23 Ajmer, India . . . . .26N 75 E
15 Akhisar, Tur. . . . . .39N 28 E
29 Akhmīm, Eg. . . . . .27N 32 E
21 Akita, Japan . . . . .40N 140 E
28 Akjoujt, Maur. 20N 15W
32 Aklavik, N.W. Ter., Can. . 68N 135W
23 Akola, India . . . . .21N 77 E
36 Akron, Ohio 41N 81W
20 Aksu, China . . . . .41N 80 E
35 Alabama (State) U.S. 33N 87W
42 Alameda, Calif. 38N 122W
43 Alamogordo, N. Mex. 33N 106W

15 Alanya, Tur. . . . . .37N 32 E
16 Alapayeysk, Russia . . . . .58N 62 E
34 Alaska (State) U.S. 65N 155W
15 Alatyr', Russia . . . . .55N 46 E
14 Albacete, Sp. . . . . .39N 2 W
15 Albania (Ctry.) Eur. . . . . .41N 20 E
48 Albany, Ga. 32N 84W
37 Albany, N.Y. 43N 74W
40 Albany, Oreg. 45N 123W
33 Albany (R.) Ont., Can. . . .52N 84W
22 Al Başrah, Iraq . . . . .30N 48 E
29 Albert, L., Ug.-Zaire. . . . . .2N 30 E
32 Alberta (Prov.) Can. 55N 117W
13 Albi, Fr. . . . . .44N 2 E
12 Ålborg, Den. . . . . .57N 10 E
43 Albuquerque, N. Mex. 35N 107W
22 Al Buraymī, Oman . . . . . .24N 56 E
22 Alcázar de San Juan, Sp. . 39N 3W
14 Alcoy, Sp. . . . . .39N 1 W
17 Aldan, Russia . . . . .59N 125 E
17 Aldanskaya, Russia . . . . .62N 135 E
17 Aleksandrovsk, Russia . . .51N 142 E
22 Aleppo, Syr. . . . . .36N 37 E
13 Alès, Fr. . . . . .44N 4 E
13 Alessandria, It. . . . . .45N 9 E
34 Aleutian Is., Alsk. 52N 175W
29 Alexandria (Al
        Iskandarīyah), Eg. . . .31N 30 E
47 Alexandria, La. 31N 92W
37 Alexandria, Va. 39N 77W
29 Alexandroúpolis, Grc. . . . .41N 26 E
29 Al Fāshir, Sud. . . . . .14N 25 E
29 Al Fayyūm, Eg. . . . . .29N 31 E
28 Algeria (Ctry.) Afr. . . . . . .29N 1 E
13 Alghero, It. . . . . .41N 8 E
28 Algiers (El Djazaïr), Alg. . 37N 3 E
22 Al Ḥawtah, Yemen . . . . . .16N 48 E
22 Al Hudaydu, Yemen . . . . .15N 43 E
22 Al Hufūf, Sau. Ar. . . . . . .25N 50 E
14 Alicante, Sp. 38N 0
26 Alice Springs, Austl. . . . . .24S 134 E
23 Aligarh, India . . . . .28N 78 E
37 Aliquippa, Pa. 41N 80W
15 Al Ismā'īlīyah, Eg. . . . . . .31N 32 E
22 Al Jawf, Sau. Ar. . . . . . . .30N 39 E
15 Al Jīzah, Eg. . . . . .30N 31 E
22 Al Khābūrah, Oman . . . . .24N 57 E
29 Al Kharṭūm Baḥrī, Sud. . .16N 33 E
22 Al Khums, Libya . . . . . . .33N 14 E
22 Al Khurmah, Sau. Ar. . . . .22N 42 E
22 Al Lādhiqīyah (Latakia),
        Syr. . . . . .36N 36 E
23 Allāhābād, India . . . . .26N 82 E
17 Allaykha, Russia . . . . . . .71N 149 E
37 Allegheny (R.) U.S. 42N 79W
37 Allentown, Pa. 41N 75W
23 Alleppey, India . . . . .10N 76 E
38 Alliance, Nebr. 42N 103W
36 Alliance, Ohio 41N 81W
22 Al Luḥayyah, Yemen . . . . .16N 43 E
22 Alma-Ata (Almaty), Kaz. . 43N 77 E
22 Al Madīnah, Sau. Ar. . . . .24N 40 E

15 Al Maḥallah al Kubrā, Eg. 31N 31 E
22 Al Manāmah, Bahrain . . . .26N 51 E'
29 Al Mansūrah, Eg. . . . . . . .31N 31 E
22 Al Mawşil, Iraq . . . . .36N 41 E
14 Almería, Sp. 37N 2W
22 Al Minyā, Eg. . . . . .28N 31 E
22 Al Mubarraz, Sau. Ar. . . . .23N 46 E
22 Al Mukallā, Yemen . . . . . .14N 49 E
22 Al Mukhā (Mocha), Yemen
                . . . . .14N 43 E
24 Alor Setar, Mala. . . . . . . .6N 100 E
36 Alpena, Mich. 45N 83W
13 Alps (Mts.) Eur. . . . . . . .46N 9 E
29 Al Qaḍārif, Sud. . . . . . . .14N 35 E
22 Al Qaṭīf, Sau. Ar. . . . . . .27N 50 E
22 Al Qayşūmah, Sau. Ar. . . .28N 46 E
22 Al Qunfudhah, Sau. Ar. . . .19N 41 E
20 Altai Mts., Asia . . . . .49N 87 E
13 Altamura, It. . . . . .41N 17 E
20 Altay, China . . . . .48N 88 E
52 Altiplano (Plateau) Bol. . .19S 68W
45 Alton, Ill. 39N 90W
37 Altoona, Pa. 40N 78W
29 Al Ubayyid, Sud. . . . . . . .13N 30 E
15 Al Uqsur (Luxor), Eg. . . . .26N 33 E
22 Al Wajh, Sau. Ar. . . . . . .26N 37 E
23 Alwar, India . . . . .28N 77 E
44 Amarillo, Tex. 35N 102W
53 Amazonas (Amazon) (R.)
        S.A. 2S 53W
31 Ambāla, India . . . . .31N 77 E
17 Ambarchik, Russia . . . . . .70N 162 E
52 Ambato, Ec. 1S 79W
8 American Samoa (Ctry.),
        Pac. O. 15S 170W
48 Americus, Ga. 32N 84W
32 Amery, Man., Can. 57N 94W
32 Amga, Russia . . . . .61N 132 E
13 Amiens, Fr. . . . . .50N 2 E
22 'Ammān, Jor. . . . . .32N 36 E
23 Amrāvati, India . . . . .21N 78 E
23 Amritsar, India . . . . .32N 75 E
37 Amsterdam, Neth. . . . . . .52N 5 E
37 Amsterdam, N.Y. 43N 74W
22 Amu Darya (R.) Asia . . . .40N 62 E
17 Amur (R.) China-Russia . .52N 126 E
41 Anaconda, Mont. 46N 113W
17 Anadyr', Russia . . . . .65N 177 E
52 Anan'yiv, Ukr. . . . . .48N 30 E
34 Anchorage, Alsk. 61N 150W
13 Ancona, It. . . . . .44N 14 E
24 Andaman Is., India . . . . . .12N 92 E
24 Andaman Sea, Asia . . . . . .13N 95 E
36 Anderson, Ind. 40N 86W
48 Anderson, S.C. 34N 83W
52 Andes Mts., S.A. 11S 75W
16 Andizhan, Uzb. . . . . .41N 73 E
21 Andong, Kor. . . . . .37N 129 E
14 Andorra (Ctry.) Eur. . . . . .42N 1 E
13 Andria, It. . . . . .41N 16 E
17 Angarsk, Russia . . . . .53N 104 E

52 Angel, Salto (Falls) Ven. .6N 62W
13 Angers, Fr. . . . . .47N 1 W
30 Angola (Ctry.) Afr. . . . . . .12S 18 E
13 Angoulême, Fr. 46N 0
51 Anguilla (Ctry.) N.A. 18N 63W
20 Ankang, China . . . . .33N 109 E
15 Ankara (Angora), Tur. . . . .40N 33 E
28 Annaba, Alg. . . . . .37N 8 E
22 An Nafūd (Des.) Sau. Ar. . 28N 40 E
22 An Najaf, Iraq . . . . .31N 45 E
24 Annamese Cordillera (Mts.)
        Laos-Viet. . . . . .18N 106 E
37 Annapolis, Md. 39N 76W
36 Ann Arbor, Mich. 42N 84W
48 Anniston, Ala. 34N 86W
21 Anqing, China . . . . .31N 117 E
20 Anshun, China . . . . .26N 106 E
15 Antakya, Tur. . . . . .36N 36 E
15 Antalya (Adalia), Tur. . . . .37N 31 E
31 Antananarivo, Mad. . . . . .19S 48 E
8 Antarctica 90S 60W
14 Antequera, Sp. . . . . .37N 5 W
51 Antigua and Barbuda
        (Ctry.) N.A. 17N 62W
54 Antofagasta, Chile 24S 70W
54 Antofalla, Salar de (Dry L.)
        Arg. 26S 67W
31 Antsiranana, Mad. . . . . . .12S 49 E
13 Antwerp, Bel. . . . . .51N 4 E
20 Anxi, China . . . . .41N 96 E
16 Anzhero-Sudzhensk, Russia
                . . . . .56N 86 E
21 Aomori, Japan . . . . .41N 141 E
6 Apeldoorn, Neth. . . . . . . .52N 6 E
35 Appalachian Mts., Can.-
        U.S. 38N 80W
13 Appennino (Mts.) It. . . . . .44N 12 E
39 Appleton, Wis. 44N 88W
15 Aqaba, Gulf of, Afr.-Asia . 28N 35 E
16 Aqmola, Kaz. . . . . .51N 72 E
11 Aqtöbe, Kaz. . . . . .50N 57 E
18 Arabian Sea, Asia . . . . . . .18N 63 E
53 Aracaju, Braz. 11S 37W
53 Araçatuba, Braz. 21S 50W
25 Arafura Sea, Austl.-Indon. .9S 133 E
53 Araguari, Braz. 19S 48W
22 Arak, Iran . . . . .34N 50 E
16 Aral, Kaz. . . . . .47N 62 E
11 Aral Sea (L.) Kaz.-Uzb. . .45N 60 E
53 Araraquara, Braz. 22S 48W
13 Arcachon, Fr. . . . . .45N 1 W
4 Arctic Ocean 80N 150W
22 Ardabīl, Iran . . . . .38N 48 E
13 Ardennes (Mts.) Bel. . . . . .50N 5 E
45 Ardmore, Okla. 34N 97W
51 Arecibo, P.R. 18N 67W
52 Arequipa, Peru 16S 71W
13 Arezzo, It. . . . . .43N 12 E
54 Argentina (Ctry.) S.A. . . .39S 67W
12 Århus, Den. . . . . .56N 10 E
34 Arizona (State) U.S. 34N 112W
44 Arkansas (R.) U.S. 35N 95W

56 *Arkansas (State) U.S.*

35 Arkansas (State) U.S. 35N 94W
11 Arkhangelsk (Archangel), Russia 64N 40 E
47 Arlington, Tex. 33N 97W
37 Arlington, Va. 39N 77W
11 Armavir, Russia 45N 41 E
11 Armenia (Ctry.) Asia 40N 45 E
52 Armenia, Col. 5N 76W
13 Arnhem, Neth. 52N 6 E
13 Arras, Fr. 50N 3 E
17 Arsen'yev, Russia 44N 134 E
15 Árta, Grc. 39N 21 E
17 Artëm, Russia 43N 132 E
51 Aruba (Ctry.) N.A. 12N 70W
16 Arys, Kaz. 42N 68 E
23 Asansol, India 24N 87 E
11 Asbest, Russia 57N 61 E
49 Asheville, N.C. 36N 83W
16 Ashkhabad, Turk. 38N 58 E
36 Ashland, Ky. 38N 83W
22 Ash Shaqrā, Sau. Ar. 25N 45 E
22 Ash Shiḥr, Yemen 15N 50 E
36 Ashtabula, Ohio 42N 81W
11 Asia Minor (Reg.) Tur. 38N 33 E
29 Asmera, Erit. 15N 39 E
29 As Sallūm, Eg. 32N 25 E
32 Assiniboia, Sask., Can. 50N 106W
22 As Sulaymānīyah, Iraq 36N 45 E
15 As Suwaydā', Syr. 33N 37 E
13 Asti, It. 45N 8 E
40 Astoria, Oreg. 46N 124W
11 Astrakhan', Russia 46N 48 E
54 Asunción, Par. 25S 57W
29 Aswān, Eg. 24N 33 E
29 Asyūṭ, Eg. 27N 31 E
29 'Atbarah, Sud. 18N 30 E
16 Atbasar, Kaz. 52N 68 E
45 Atchison, Kans. 40N 95W
32 Athabasca, Alta., Can. 55N 113W
32 Athabasca (L.) Can. 59N 109W
32 Athabasca (R.) Alta., Can. 57N 112W
48 Athens, Ga. 34N 83W
15 Athens (Athínai), Grc. 38N 24 E
48 Atlanta, Ga. 34N 84W
37 Atlantic City, N.J. 39N 74W
8 Atlantic Ocean 20N 40W
38 Atlas Mts., Afr. 33N 2W
32 Atlin (L.) Can. 60N 133W
22 Aṭ Ṭā'if, Sau. Ar. 21N 41 E
37 Attleboro, Mass. 42N 71W
22 Aṭ Ṭurayf, Sau. Ar. 32N 38 E
11 Atyraū, Kaz. 47N 52 E
37 Auburn, Maine 44N 70W
27 Auckland, N.Z. 37S 175 E
13 Augsburg, Ger. 48N 11 E
49 Augusta, Ga. 33N 82W
35 Augusta, Maine 44N 70W
23 Aurangābād, India 20N 76 E
13 Aurillac, Fr. 45N 2 E
36 Aurora, Ill. 42N 88W
47 Austin, Tex. 30N 98W
26 Australia (Ctry.) Pac. O. 25S 135 E
13 Austria (Ctry.) Eur. 47N 13 E
13 Avignon, Fr. 44N 5 E
16 Ayaköz, Kaz. 48N 80 E
17 Ayan, Russia 56N 138 E
15 Aydin, Tur. 38N 28 E
29 Aysha, Eth. 11N 43 E
11 Azerbaijan (Ctry.) Asia 40N 47 E
28 Azores (Açores) (Is.) Port. 38N 29W
15 Azov, Sea of, Russia-Ukr. 46N 36 E
22 Aẓ Ẓahrān (Dhahran), Sau. Ar. 26N 50 E
29 Az Zaqāzīq, Eg. 31N 32 E

B

31 Baadheere, Som. 2N 42 E
29 Babanūsah, Sud. 12N 28 E
22 Bābol, Iran 36N 53 E
22 Babylon (Ruins) Iraq 32N 45 E
15 Bacău, Rom. 47N 27 E
20 Bachu, China 40N 78 E
24 Bac Lieu, Viet. 10N 106 E
24 Bacolod, Phil. 11N 123 E
13 Baden-Baden, Ger. 49N 8 E
33 Baffin I., N.W. Ter., Can. 67N 69W
22 Bāfq, Iran 32N 55 E
54 Bagé, Braz. 31S 54W
22 Baghdād, Iraq 33N 44 E
24 Bago, Burma 17N 96 E
25 Baguio, Phil. 16N 121 E
51 Bahamas (Ctry.) N.A. 27N 77W
23 Bahāwalpur, Pak. 29N 72 E
54 Bahía Blanca, Arg. 39S 62W
22 Bahrain (Ctry.) Asia 26N 51 E
15 Baia-Mare, Rom. 48N 24 E
40 Baker, Oreg. 45N 118W
32 Baker (L.) N.W. Ter., Can. 64N 96W
42 Bakersfield, Calif. 35N 119W
22 Bakhtarān, Iran 34N 47 E
11 Baku (Bakı), Azer. 40N 50 E
11 Balashov, Russia 51N 43 E
28 Baleares, Islas (Is.) Sp. 39N 3 E
33 Baleine, Grande R. de la (R.) Que., Can. 55N 76W
24 Bali (I.) Indon. 8S 115 E
15 Balikesir, Tur. 40N 28 E
16 Balkhash, Lake, see Balqash kölī (L.) Kaz. 47N 75 E
27 Ballarat, Austl. 38S 144 E
16 Balqash, Kaz. 47N 75 E
16 Balqash kölī, Kaz. 47N 75 E
50 Balsas (R.) Mex. 18N 101W
15 Balta, Ukr. 48N 30W
15 Bălţi, Mol. 48N 28 E
12 Baltic Sea, Eur. 55N 17 E
37 Baltimore, Md. 39N 77W
28 Bamako, Mali 13N 8W
13 Bamberg, Ger. 50N 11 E
22 Bampūr, Iran 27N 60 E
23 Bānda, India 26N 80 E
25 Banda, Laut (Banda Sea), Indon. 6S 127 E
22 Bandar-e 27N 56 E
22 Bandar-e Anzalī, Iran 37N 49 E
22 Bandar-e Būshehr, Iran 29N 51 E
22 Bandar-e Khomeynī, Iran 30N 49 E
22 Bandar-e Torkeman, Iran 37N 54 E
15 Bandirma, Tur. 40N 28 E
24 Bandung, Indon. 7S 107 E
23 Bangalore, India 13N 75 E
29 Banghāzī (Bengasi), Libya 32N 20 E
24 Bangkok (Krung Thep), Thai. 14N 100 E
23 Bangladesh (Ctry.) Asia 24N 90 E
29 Bangui, Cen. Afr. Rep. 4N 19 E
30 Bangweulu, L., Zambia 12S 30 E
29 Banī Suwayf, Eg. 29N 31 E
15 Banja Luka, Bos. 45N 17 E
24 Banjarmasin, Indon. 3S 115 E
28 Banjul, Gam. 13N 17W
21 Baotou, China 40N 110 E
31 Baraawe, Som. 1N 44 E
10 Baranovichi, Bela. 53N 26 E
53 Barbacena, Braz. 21S 44W
51 Barbados (Ctry.) N.A. 14N 60W
36 Barberton, Ohio 41N 82W
14 Barcelona, Sp. 41N 2 E
23 Bareilly, India 28N 79 E
13 Bari, It. 41N 17 E
20 Barkol, China 44N 93 E
13 Barletta, It. 41N 16 E
16 Barnaul, Russia 53N 83 E
23 Baroda, India 22N 73 E
52 Barquisimeto, Ven. 10N 69W
52 Barrancabermeja, Col. 7N 74W
52 Barranquilla, Col. 11N 75W
14 Barreiro, Port. 39N 9W
32 Barrhead, Alta., Can. 54N 114W
12 Barrow-in-Furness, Eng. 54N 3W
13 Basel, Switz. 48N 8 E
51 Basse Terre, Guad. 16N 62W
27 Bass Str., Austl. 40S 145 E
13 Bastia, Fr. 43N 9 E
28 Bata, Eq. Gui. 2N 10 E
20 Batang, China 30N 99 E
25 Batangas, Phil. 14N 121 E
24 Bătdâmbâng, Camb. 13N 103 E
13 Bath, Eng. 51N 2W
28 Batna, Alg. 36N 6 E
47 Baton Rouge, La. 30N 91W
36 Battle Creek, Mich. 42N 85W
11 Batumi, Geor. 42N 41 E
25 Bauang, Phil. 17N 120 E
53 Bauru, Braz. 22S 49W
25 Bay, Laguna de (L.) Phil. 14N 121 E
36 Bay City, Mich. 44N 84W
31 Baydhabo, Som. 3N 44 E
17 Baykal, Ozero (L. Baikal), Russia 53N 109 E
17 Baykit, Russia 62N 97 E
13 Bayonne, Fr. 43N 1W
37 Bayonne, N.J. 41N 74W
16 Bayqongyr, Kaz. 48N 66 E
45 Beatrice, Nebr. 40N 97W
47 Beaumont, Tex. 30N 94W
13 Bedford, Eng. 52N 0
20 Beihai, China 21N 109 E
21 Beijing (Peking), China 40N 116 E
22 Beirut, Leb. 34N 35 E
14 Beja, Tun. 37N 9 E
28 Bejaïa, Alg. 37N 5 E
10 Belarus (Ctry.) Eur. 53N 28 E
33 Belcher Is., N.W. Ter., Can. 56N 79W
53 Belém (Pará), Braz. 1S 48W
12 Belfast, N. Ire. 55N 6W
13 Belfort, Fr. 48N 7 E
13 Belgium (Ctry.) Eur. 51N 3 E
15 Belgrade (Beograd), Yugo. 45N 21 E
50 Belize (Ctry.) N.A. 17N 89W
50 Belize City, Belize 17N 88W
23 Bellary, India 15N 77 E
33 Belle Isle, Str. of, Can. 51N 56W
40 Bellingham, Wash. 49N 122W
50 Belmopan, Belize 16N 89W
17 Belogorsk, Russia 51N 129 E
53 Belo Horizonte, Braz. 20S 44W
39 Beloit, Wis. 43N 89W
11 Beloretsk, Russia 54N 58 E
40 Bend, Oreg. 44N 121W
31 Bender Beyla, Som. 9N 51 E
13 Benevento, It. 41N 15 E
18 Bengal, Bay of, Asia 18N 88 E
21 Bengbu, China 33N 117 E
28 Benin (Ctry.) Afr. 8N 2 E
28 Benin, Bight of (B.) Afr. 5N 2 E
28 Benin City, Nig. 6N 6 E
28 Beni Saf, Alg. 35N 1W
30 Benoni, S. Afr. 26S 28 E
28 Benue (R.) Cam.-Nig. 8N 8 E
31 Berbera, Som. 10N 45 E
10 Berdychiv, Ukr. 50N 29 E
16 Berëzovo, Russia 64N 65 E
13 Bergamo, It. 46N 10 E
12 Bergen, Nor. 60N 5 E
23 Berhampur, India 19N 85 E
19 Bering Sea, Asia-N.A. 58N 179W
42 Berkeley, Calif. 38N 122W
13 Berlin, Ger. 52N 13 E
51 Bermuda (Ctry.) N.A. 32N 65W
13 Bern, Switz. 47N 7 E
54 Bernal, Arg. 34S 58W
36 Berwyn, Ill. 42N 88W
13 Besançon, Fr. 47N 6 E
28 Beskra, Alg. 35N 6 E
48 Bessemer, Ala. 33N 87W
34 Bethel, Alsk. 61N 162W
37 Bethelehem, Pa. 41N 75W
15 Bethlehem, Isr. Occ. 32N 35 E
37 Beverly, Mass. 43N 71W
15 Beyşehir Gölü (L.) Tur. 38N 32 E
11 Bezhitsa, Russia 53N 34 E
13 Béziers, Fr. 43N 3 E
23 Bhāgalpur, India 25N 87 E
23 Bhātpāra, India 23N 89 E
23 Bhaunagar, India 22N 73 E
23 Bhopāl, India 23N 77 E
23 Bhuj, India 24N 70 E
23 Bhutan (Ctry.) Asia 27N 90 E
28 Biafra, Bight of (B.) Afr. 3N 9 E
12 Bialystok, Pol. 53N 23 E
13 Bielefeld, Ger. 52N 9 E
33 Bienville, Lac (L.) Que., Can. 56N 73W
23 Bilāspur, India 22N 82 E
14 Bilbao, Sp. 43N 3W
41 Billings, Mont. 46N 108W
48 Biloxi, Miss. 30N 89W
37 Binghamton, N.Y. 42N 76W
28 Bioko (I.) Eq. Gui. 3N 8 E
15 Bîrlad, Rom. 46N 28 E
48 Birmingham, Ala. 34N 87W
13 Birmingham, Eng. 52N 2W
17 Birobidzhan, Russia 49N 133 E
16 Birsk, Russia 55N 55 E
43 Bisbee, Ariz. 31N 110W
14 Biscay, B. of, Fr.-Sp. 45N 3W
16 Bishkek, Kyrg. 43N 75 E
30 Bisho, Ciskei 33N 27W
38 Bismarck, N. Dak. 47N 101W
28 Bissau, Gui-B. 12N 16W
15 Bitola, Mac. 41N 21 E
40 Bitterroot Range, U.S. 47N 115W
16 Biysk, Russia 53N 85 E
28 Bizerte, Tun. 37N 10 E
38 Black Hills, U.S. 44N 104W
15 Black Sea, Eur. 43N 33 E
17 Blagoveshchensk, Russia 50N 128 E
54 Blanca, B., Arg. 39S 61W
30 Blantyre, Malawi 16S 35 E
30 Bloemfontein, S. Afr. 29S 26 E
13 Blois, Fr. 48N 1 E
36 Bloomington, Ind. 39N 87W
40 Blue Mts., U.S. 46N 118W
29 Blue Nile (R.) Eth.-Sud. 12N 34 E
35 Blue Ridge, U.S. 37N 81W
28 Bobo-Dioulasso, Burkina 11N 4W
10 Bobruysk, Bela. 53N 29 E
17 Bodaybo, Russia 57N 115 E
13 Boden See (L.) Ger.-Switz. 48N 9 E
24 Bogor, Indon. 7S 107 E
52 Bogotá, see Santa Fe de Bogotá, Col. 5N 74W
17 Bogotol, Russia 56N 89 E
21 Bo Hai (B.) China 39N 119 E
13 Bohemian Forest (Mts.) Ger.-Czech. 50N 12 E
40 Boise, Idaho 44N 116W
32 Boissevain, Man., Can. 49N 100W
52 Bolivia (Ctry.) S.A. 17S 64W
13 Bologna, It. 44N 11 E
13 Bolzano, It. 46N 11 E
23 Bombay, India 19N 73 E
28 Bomi Hills, Lib. 7N 11W
29 Bomongo, Zaire 2N 18 E
13 Bonn, Ger. 51N 7 E
31 Boorama, Som. 10N 43 E
31 Boosaaso, Som. 11N 49 E
32 Boothia Pen., N.W. Ter., Can. 71N 94W
30 Bophuthatswana (Ctry.) Afr. 26S 26 E
12 Borås, Swe. 58N 13 E
22 Borāzjān, Iran 29N 51 E
13 Bordeaux, Fr. 45N 1W
14 Bordj-Bou-Arreridj, Alg. 36N 5 E
11 Borisoglebsk, Russia 51N 42 E
24 Borneo (I.) Asia 1N 113 E
16 Borovichi, Russia 58N 34 E
31 Borraan, Som. 10N 49 E
22 Borūjerd, Iran 34N 49 E
17 Borzya, Russia 51N 117 E
21 Boshan, China 37N 118 E
15 Bosnia and Herzegovina (Ctry.) Eur. 44N 18 E
37 Boston, Mass. 42N 71W
12 Bothnia, Gulf of, Fin.-Swe. 62N 19 E
15 Botosani, Rom. 48N 27 E
30 Botswana (Ctry.) Afr. 22S 23 E
28 Bouaké, C. Iv. 8N 5W
44 Boulder, Colo. 40N 105W
42 Boulder City, Nev. 36N 115W
13 Bourges, Fr. 47N 2 E
36 Bowling Green, Ohio 41N 84W
41 Bozeman, Mont. 46N 111W
12 Bradford, Eng. 54N 2W
14 Braga, Port. 42N 8W
23 Brahmaputra (R.) Asia 27N 92 E
15 Brăila, Rom. 45N 28 E
13 Brandenburg, Ger. 52N 13 E
32 Brandon, Man., Can. 50N 100W
53 Brasília, Braz. 16S 48W
15 Braşov, Rom. 46N 26 E
13 Bratislava, Slov. 48N 17 E
17 Bratsk, Russia 56N 101 E
13 Braunschweig, Ger. 52N 11 E
42 Brawley, Calif. 33N 116W
53 Brazil (Ctry.) S.A. 8S 60W
30 Brazzaville, Congo 4S 15 E
13 Bremen, Ger. 53N 9 E
13 Bremerhaven, Ger. 54N 9 E
40 Bremerton, Wash. 48N 123W
13 Brenner P., Aus.-It. 47N 11 E
13 Brescia, It. 46N 10 E
13 Brest, Fr. 48N 4W
10 Brest, Bela. 52N 24 E
37 Bridgeport, Conn. 41N 73W
51 Bridgetown, Barb. 13N 60W
13 Brig, Switz. 46N 8 E
13 Brighton, Eng. 51N 0
27 Brisbane, Austl. 27S 153 E
13 Bristol, Eng. 51N 3W
49 Bristol, Tenn. 37N 82W
13 Bristol Chan., U.K. 51N 4W
32 British Columbia (Prov.) Can. 56N 126W
12 British Isles, Eur. 55N 4W
13 Brno, Czech. 49N 17 E
37 Brockton, Mass. 42N 71W
47 Brownsville, Tex. 26N 97W
46 Brownwood, Tex. 32N 99W
13 Brugge, Bel. 51N 3 E
24 Brunei (Ctry.) Asia 5N 114 E
49 Brunswick, Ga. 31N 81W
13 Brussels, Bel. 51N 4 E
11 Bryansk, Russia 53N 34 E
52 Bucaramanga, Col. 7N 73W
15 Bucharest, Rom. 44N 26 E
13 Budapest, Hung. 47N 19 E
52 Buenaventura, Col. 4N 77W
54 Buenos Aires, Arg. 34S 58W
54 Buenos Aires (L.) Arg.-Chile 46S 72W
37 Buffalo, N.Y. 43N 79W
12 Bug (R.) Eur. 52N 21 E
16 Bugul'ma, Russia 55N 53 E
30 Bujumbura, Burundi 3S 29 E
30 Bukavu, Zaire 3S 29 E
16 Bukhara, Uzb. 40N 64 E
25 Bula, Indon. 3S 130 E
30 Bulawayo, Zimb. 20S 29 E
15 Bulgaria (Ctry.) Eur. 43N 25 E
17 Bulun, Russia 71N 127 E
25 Buna, Pap. N. Gui. 9S 148 E
22 Buraydah, Sau. Ar. 26N 44 E
31 Burco, Som. 9N 45 E
23 Burdwān, India 23N 88 E
17 Bureya, Russia 50N 130 E
15 Burgas, Bul. 42N 27 E
14 Burgos, Sp. 42N 4W
23 Burhānpur, India 21N 76 E
28 Burkina Faso (Ctry.) Afr. 13N 3W
39 Burlington, Iowa 41N 91W
37 Burlington, Vt. 44N 73W
20 Burma see Myanmar (Ctry.) Asia 22N 95 E
15 Bursa, Tur. 40N 28 E
29 Būr Sūdān, Sud. 19N 37 E
30 Burundi (Ctry.) Afr. 3S 30 E
37 Butler, Pa. 41N 80W
41 Butte, Mont. 46N 113W
31 Buulo Berde, Som. 4N 46 E
16 Buy, Russia 58N 42 E
15 Buzău, Rom. 45N 27 E
16 Buzuluk, Russia 53N 52 E
12 Bydgoszcz, Pol. 53N 18 E
13 Bytom, Pol. 50N 19 E

C

52 Cabimas, Ven. 10N 71W
30 Cabinda, Ang. 6S 12 E
14 Cáceres, Sp. 39N 6W
53 Cachoeiro do Itapemirim, Braz. 21S 41W
31 Cadale, Som. 3N 46 E
14 Cádiz, Sp. 37N 6W
13 Caen, Fr. 49N 0
13 Cagliari, It. 39N 9 E
51 Caguas, P.R. 18N 66W
29 Cairo (Al Qāhirah), Eg. 30N 31 E
36 Cairo, Ill. 37N 89W
28 Calabar, Nig. 5N 8 E
13 Calais, Fr. 51N 2 E
15 Călărasi, Rom. 44N 27 E
23 Calcutta, India 23N 88 E
42 Calexico, Calif. 33N 115W
32 Calgary, Alta., Can. 51N 114W
52 Cali, Col. 3N 76W
23 Calicut, India 11N 76 E
34 California (State) U.S. 38N 121W
50 California, G. de, Mex. 26N 110W
52 Callao, Peru 13S 77W
13 Caltanissetta, It. 37N 14 E
31 Caluula, Som. 12N 51 E
51 Camagüey, Cuba 21N 78W
24 Cambodia (Ctry.) Asia 12N 104 E
13 Cambridge, Eng. 52N 0
13 Cambrai, Fr. 50N 3 E
37 Cambridge, Mass. 42N 71W
37 Camden, N.J. 40N 75W
28 Cameroon (Ctry.) Afr. 5N 12 E
50 Campeche, Mex. 19N 90W
54 Campinas, Braz. 23S 47W
53 Campo Grande, Braz. 20S 55W
53 Campos, Braz. 22S 41W
32 Canada (Ctry.) N.A. 55N 100W
44 Canadian (R.) U.S. 35N 97W
15 Çanakkale Boğazı (Dardanelles) (Str.) Tur. 40N 26 E
28 Canarias, Islas (Canary Is.), Sp. 29N 18W
49 Canaveral, C., Fla. 28N 81W
27 Canberra, Austl. 35S 149 E
33 Caniapiscau (R.) Que., Can. 57N 69W
13 Cannes, Fr. 44N 7 E

Erzgebirge (Ore Mts.), Ger.-Czech. 57

36 Canton, Ohio 41N 81W
45 Cape Girardeau, Mo. 37N 90W
30 Cape Town, S. Afr. 34S 18E
28 Cape Verde (Ctry.) Afr. 16N 25W
51 Cap-Haïtien, Hai. 20N 72W
30 Caprivi Strip (Reg.) Nam. 18S 23E
52 Caracas, Ven. 10N 67W
53 Caravelas, Braz. 18S 39W
13 Carcassonne, Fr. 43N 2E
13 Cardiff, Wales 51N 3W
51 Caribbean Sea, N.A.-S.A. 15N 67W
32 Cariboo Mts., B.C., Can. 54N 122W
12 Carlisle, Eng. 55N 3W
15 Carpathians (Mts.) Eur. 49N 22E
26 Carpentaria, Gulf of, Austl. 15S 138E
13 Carrara, It. 44N 10E
42 Carson City, Nev. 39N 120W
52 Cartagena, Col. 10N 76W
14 Cartagena, Sp. 38N 1W
14 Carthage, Tun. 37N 10E
53 Caruaru, Braz. 8S 36W
28 Casablanca, Mor. 34N 8W
40 Cascade Ra., N.A. 44N 122W
31 Caseyr (C.) Som. 12N 51E
41 Casper, Wyo. 43N 106W
11 Caspian Sea, Asia-Europe 42N 49E
14 Castellón de la Plana, Sp. 40N 0
54 Catamarca, Arg. 28S 66W
13 Catania, It. 37N 15E
11 Caucasus (Mts.), Asia-Europe 43N 42E
54 Caxias do Sul, Braz. 29S 51W
53 Cayenne, Fr. Gui. 5N 52W
25 Cebu, Phil. 10N 124E
32 Cedar (L.) Man., Can. 53N 101W
39 Cedar Rapids, Iowa 42N 92W
31 Ceel Buur, Som. 5N 47E
13 Cegléd, Hung. 47N 20E
24 Celebes (Sulawesi) (I.) Indon. 2S 120E
24 Celebes Sea, Asia 4N 122E
13 Celle, Ger. 53N 10E
52 Central, Cordillera (Ra.) Bol. 21S 65W
29 Central African Republic (Ctry.) Afr. 7N 20E
13 České Budějovice, Czech. 49N 14E
14 Ceuta, Sp. N. Afr. 36N 5W
29 Chad (Ctry.) Afr. 15N 17E
29 Chad, L., Afr. 14N 14E
13 Chalon-sur-Saône, Fr. 47N 5E
23 Chaman, Pak. 31N 66E
36 Champaign, Ill. 40N 88W
37 Champlain, L., Can.-U.S. 45N 73W
21 Changchun, China 44N 125E
21 Changde, China 29N 112E
21 Changsha, China 28N 113E
21 Changzhou, China 32N 120E
13 Channel Is., Eur. 49N 3W
24 Chanthaburi, Thai. 13N 102E
45 Chanute, Kans. 38N 95W
21 Chao'an, China 24N 117E
24 Chao Phraya (R.) Thai. 14N 100E
50 Chapala, Lago de (L.) Mex. 20N 103W
49 Chapel Hill, N.C. 36N 79W
16 Chardzhou, Turk. 39N 64E
13 Charleroi, Bel. 50N 5E
49 Charleston, S.C. 33N 80W
36 Charleston, W. Va. 38N 82W
49 Charlotte, N.C. 35N 81W
51 Charlotte Amalie (St. Thomas), Vir. Is. 18N 65W
37 Charlottesville, Va. 38N 78W
33 Charlottetown, P.E.I., Can. 46N 63W
13 Châteauroux, Fr. 47N 2E
13 Châtellerault, Fr. 47N 1E
48 Chattanooga, Tenn. 35N 85W
24 Chau-phu, Camb. 11N 105E
11 Cheboksary, Russia 56N 47E
13 Chełm, Pol. 51N 23E
37 Chelsea, Mass. 42N 71W
16 Chelyabinsk, Russia 55N 61E
13 Chemnitz, Ger. 51N 13E
21 Chengde, China 41N 118E
20 Chengdu, China 30N 104E
13 Cherbourg, Fr. 50N 2W
16 Cherdyn', Russia 60N 56E
16 Cherepanovo, Russia 54N 83E
11 Cherepovets, Russia 59N 38E
11 Chernihiv, Ukr. 51N 31E
10 Chernivtsi, Ukr. 48N 26E
12 Chernyakhovsk, Russia 55N 22E
37 Chesapeake Bay, U.S. 38N 76W
16 Chesnokovka, Russia 53N 84E
37 Chester, Pa. 40N 75W
32 Chesterfield Inlet, N.W. Ter., Can. 63N 91W
44 Cheyenne, Wyo. 41N 105W
24 Chiang Rai, Thai. 20N 100E
33 Chibougamau, Que., Can. 50N 74W
36 Chicago, Ill. 42N 88W
36 Chicago Heights, Ill. 41N 88W
44 Chickasha, Okla. 35N 98W
52 Chiclayo, Peru 7S 80W
37 Chicopee, Mass. 42N 73W
33 Chicoutimi, Que., Can. 48N 71W
13 Chieti, It. 42N 14E
21 Chifeng, China 42N 119E
50 Chihuahua, Mex. 29N 106W
22 Chikishlyar, Turk. 38N 54E
54 Chile (Ctry.) S.A. 38S 72W
54 Chillán, Chile 37S 72W
36 Chillicothe, Ohio 39N 83W
21 Chilung, Taiwan 25N 122E
52 Chimbote, Peru 9S 78W
16 Chimkent, see Shymkent, Kaz. 42N 70E
20 China (Ctry.) Asia 34N 101E
30 Chingola, Zambia 13S 28E
16 Chistopol', Russia 55N 50E
17 Chita, Russia 52N 114E
23 Chitrāl, Pak. 36N 72E
23 Chittagong, Bngl. 22N 91E
21 Chŏngjin, Kor. 42N 130E
20 Chongqing, China 30N 107E
21 Choybalsan, Mong. 48N 114E
27 Christchurch, N.Z. 43S 173E
24 Christmas I. (Ctry.) Ind. O. 10S 105E
17 Chumikan, Russia 55N 135E
54 Chuquicamata, Chile 22S 69W
32 Churchill, Man., Can. 59N 94W
32 Churchill (R.) Can. 58N 95W
11 Chusovoy, Russia 58N 58E
16 Chust, Uzb. 41N 71E
36 Cicero, Ill. 42N 88W
15 Cide, Tur. 42N 33E
52 Ciénaga, Col. 11N 74W
51 Cienfuegos, Cuba 22N 80W
36 Cincinnati, Ohio 39N 84W
24 Cirebon, Indon. 7S 109E
30 Ciskei (Ctry.) Afr. 33S 27E
52 Ciudad Bolívar, Ven. 8N 64W
50 Ciudad Chetumal (Payo Obispo), Mex. 18N 88W
52 Ciudad Guayana, Ven. 9N 63W
50 Ciudad Juárez, Mex. 32N 106W
50 Ciudad Obregón, Mex. 28N 110W
14 Ciudad Real, Sp. 39N 4W
50 Ciudad Victoria, Mex. 24N 99W
37 Clarksburg, W. Va. 39N 80W
49 Clearwater, Fla. 28N 83W
47 Cleburne, Tex. 32N 97W
13 Clermont-Ferrand, Fr. 46N 3E
36 Cleveland, Ohio 41N 82W
36 Cleveland Heights, Ohio 41N 82W
37 Clifton, N.J. 41N 74W
44 Clovis, N. Mex. 34N 103W
15 Cluj-Napoca, Rom. 47N 24E
32 Coast Mts., Can.-U.S. 57N 131W
34 Coast Ranges, U.S. 40N 123W
37 Cod, Cape, Mass. 42N 70W
40 Coeur d'Alene, Idaho 48N 117W
45 Coffeyville, Kans. 37N 96W
14 Coimbra, Port. 40N 8W
50 Colima, Mex. 19N 104W
13 Colmar, Fr. 49N 7E
13 Cologne (Köln), Ger. 51N 7E
52 Colombia (Ctry.) S.A. 3N 74W
23 Colombo, Sri Lanka 7N 80E
51 Colón, Pan. 9N 80W
52 Colon, Archipiélago de (Galápagos Is.), Ec. 0 90W
34 Colorado (R.) Mex.-U.S. 36N 113W
47 Colorado (R.) Tex. 30N 98W
34 Colorado (State) U.S. 39N 105W
54 Colorado, R., Arg. 39S 65W
44 Colorado Springs, Colo. 39N 105W
45 Columbia, Mo. 39N 92W
49 Columbia, S.C. 34N 81W
32 Columbia (R.) Can.-U.S. 46N 120W
48 Columbus, Ga. 32N 85W
36 Columbus, Ohio 40N 83W
23 Comilla, Bngl. 24N 91E
13 Como, It. 46N 9E
54 Comodoro Rivadavia, Arg. 46S 68W
31 Comoros (Ctry.) Afr. 12S 44E
28 Conakry, Gui. 9N 14W
54 Concepción, Chile 37S 73W
54 Concepción del Uruguay, Arg. 33S 58W
37 Concord, N.H. 43N 71W
54 Concordia, Arg. 31S 58W
30 Congo (Ctry.) Afr. 3S 14E
30 Congo (R.) Afr. 4S 16E
37 Connecticut (R.) U.S. 44N 72W
35 Connecticut (State) U.S. 42N 73W
15 Constanța, Rom. 44N 29E
28 Constantine, Alg. 36N 7E
23 Cooch Behār, India 26N 90E
12 Copenhagen (København), Den. 56N 12E
49 Coral Gables, Fla. 26N 80W
27 Coral Sea, Oc. 14S 155E
54 Córdoba, Arg. 32S 64W
50 Córdoba, Mex. 19N 97W
14 Córdoba, Sp. 38N 5W
13 Cork, Ire. 52N 8W
52 Coro, Ven. 11N 70W
47 Corpus Christi, Tex. 28N 97W
54 Corrientes, Arg. 27S 59W
13 Corsica (I.) Fr. 42N 9E
47 Corsicana, Tex. 32N 96W
15 Çorum, Tur. 41N 35E
40 Corvallis, Oreg. 45N 123W
51 Costa Rica (Ctry.) N.A. 10N 85W
28 Cote d'Ivoire (Ctry.), Afr. 7N 6W
28 Cotonou, Benin 7N 3E
13 Cottbus, Ger. 52N 14E
38 Council Bluffs, Iowa 41N 96W
36 Covington, Ky. 39N 85W
15 Craiova, Rom. 44N 24E
37 Cranston, R.I. 42N 71W
40 Crater L., Oreg. 43N 122W
13 Cremona, It. 45N 10E
15 Crete (I.) Grc. 35N 25E
11 Crimean Peninsula, see Kryms'kyy pivostriv, Ukr. 45N 34E
14 Croatia (Ctry.) Eur. 45N 15E
13 Croydon, Eng. 51N 0
51 Cuba (Ctry.) N.A. 22N 79W
52 Cúcuta, Col. 8N 72W
23 Cuddalore, India 12N 80E
23 Cuddapah, India 14N 79E
52 Cuenca, Ec. 3S 79W
50 Cuernavaca, Mex. 19N 99W
53 Cuiabá, Braz. 16S 56W
50 Culiacán, Mex. 25N 107W
14 Cullera, Sp. 39N 0
52 Cumaná, Ven. 10N 64W
54 Curico, Chile 35S 71W
54 Curitiba, Braz. 26S 49W
23 Cuttack, India 21N 86E
36 Cuyahoga Falls, Ohio 41N 81W
52 Cuzco, Peru 14S 72W
15 Cyprus (Ctry.) Asia 35N 33E
15 Cyprus, North (Ctry.) Asia 36N 33E
13 Czech Republic (Ctry.) Eur. 49N 15E
13 Częstochowa, Pol. 51N 19E

D

28 Dakar, Sen. 15N 17W
28 Dakhla, W. Sah. 24N 16W
20 Dali, China 35N 110E
21 Dalian (Lüda), China 39N 121E
47 Dallas, Tex. 33N 97W
17 Dalnerechensk, Russia 46N 134E
23 Damān, India 21N 73E
29 Damanhūr, Eg. 31N 31E
22 Damascus (Dimashq), Syr. 34N 36E
22 Dāmghān, Iran 36N 54E
24 Da Nang (Tourane), Viet. 16N 108E
21 Dandong, China 40N 124E
15 Danube (R.) Eur. 43N 24E
36 Danville, Ill. 40N 88W
49 Danville, Va. 37N 80W
12 Danzig, Gulf of, Pol.-Russia 54N 19E
23 Darbhanga, India 26N 86E
31 Dar es Salaam, Tan. 7S 39E
23 Darjeeling, India 27N 88E
27 Darling (R.) Austl. 33S 143E
26 Darling Ra., Austl. 31S 116E
13 Darmstadt, Ger. 50N 9E
29 Darnah, Libya 33N 23E
26 Darwin, Austl. 12S 131E
10 Daugavpils, Lat. 56N 26E
32 Dauphin, Man., Can. 51N 100W
25 Davao, Phil. 7N 125E
39 Davenport, Iowa 42N 91W
51 David, Pan. 8N 82W
24 Dawei, Mya. 14N 98E
32 Dawson, Yukon, Can. 64N 139W
32 Dawson Creek, B.C., Can. 56N 120W
20 Daxian, China 31N 107E
22 Dayr az Zawr, Syr. 35N 40E
36 Dayton, Ohio 40N 84W
49 Daytona Beach, Fla. 29N 81W
21 Da Yunhe (Grand Canal), China 35N 117E
15 Dead Sea, Asia 32N 35E
38 Deadwood, S. Dak. 44N 104W
36 Dearborn, Mich. 42N 83W
42 Death Valley, Calif. 36N 117W
13 Debrecen, Hung. 48N 22E
48 Decatur, Ala. 34N 87W
36 Decatur, Ill. 40N 89W
23 Deccan Plat., India 19N 77E
23 Dehra Dūn, India 30N 78E
37 Delaware (R.) U.S. 42N 75W
35 Delaware (State) U.S. 39N 75W
37 Delaware Bay, U.S. 39N 75W
23 Delhi, India 29N 77E
46 Del Rio, Tex. 29N 101W
43 Deming, N. Mex. 32N 108W
45 Denison, Tex. 34N 97W
15 Denizli, Tur. 38N 29E
12 Denmark (Ctry.) Eur. 56N 10E
44 Denver, Colo. 40N 105W
23 Dera Ghāzi Khān, Pak. 30N 71E
23 Dera Ismāīl Khān, Pak. 32N 71E
13 Derby, Eng. 53N 1W
29 Dese, Eth. 11N 40E
39 Des Moines, Iowa 42N 94W
39 Des Moines (R.) U.S. 41N 93W
36 Des Plaines, Ill. 42N 88W
13 Dessau, Ger. 52N 12E
36 Detroit, Mich. 42N 83W
38 Devils L., N. Dak. 48N 99W
22 Dezfūl, Iran 32N 49E
23 Dhaka (Dacca), Bngl. 24N 90E
23 Dhawalāgiri (Mt.) Nepal 28N 84E
23 Dhule, India 21N 75E
38 Dickinson, N. Dak. 47N 103W
13 Dijon, Fr. 47N 5E
16 Dikson, Russia 73N 80E
25 Dili, Indon. 9S 126E
29 Dire Dawa, Eth. 10N 42E
37 District of Columbia, U.S. 39N 77W
23 Diu, India 21N 71E
22 Diyarbakir, Tur. 38N 40E
14 Djerid, Chott (L.) Tun. 33N 8E
29 Djibouti, Djibouti 12N 43E
29 Djibouti (Ctry.) Afr. 12N 43E
11 Dniprodzerzhyns'k, Ukr. 48N 34E
11 Dnipropetrovs'k, Ukr. 48N 35E
15 Dnister (R.) Mol.-Ukr. 46N 30E
25 Dobo, Indon. 6S 134E
15 Dobrich, Bul. 44N 28E
44 Dodge City, Kans. 38N 100W
30 Dodoma, Tan. 6S 36E
51 Dominica (Ctry.) N.A. 15N 61W
51 Dominican Republic (Ctry.) N.A. 19N 71W
11 Don (R.) Russia 47N 39E
11 Donets'k, Ukr. 48N 38E
24 Dong Hoi, Viet. 17N 107E
31 Doolow, Som. 4N 42E
13 Dortmund, Ger. 52N 7E
48 Dothan, Ala. 31N 85W
28 Douala, Cam. 4N 10E
43 Douglas, Ariz. 31N 109W
14 Douro (Duero) (R.) Port.-Sp. 41N 8W
37 Dover, Del. 39N 75W
13 Dover, Eng. 51N 1E
13 Dover, Str. of, Eng.-Fr. 50N 1E
30 Drakensberg (Mts.) Afr. 29S 29E
15 Dráma, Grc. 41N 24E
13 Dresden, Ger. 51N 14E
10 Drohobych, Ukr. 49N 24E
32 Drumheller, Alta., Can. 51N 113W
33 Dryden, Ont., Can. 50N 93W
22 Dubayy, U.A.E. 25N 55E
12 Dublin (Baile Átha Cliath), Ire. 53N 6W
15 Dubrovnik, Cro. 43N 18E
39 Dubuque, Iowa 42N 91W
16 Dudinka, Russia 69N 86E
13 Dudley, Eng. 53N 2W
13 Duisburg, Ger. 51N 7E
39 Duluth, Minn. 47N 92W
29 Dumyāṭ (Damietta), Eg. 31N 32E
12 Dundalk, Ire. 54N 6W
37 Dundalk, Md. 39N 77W
12 Dundee, Scot. 56N 3W
27 Dunedin, N.Z. 46S 171E
12 Dun Laoghaire, Ire. 53N 6W
50 Durango, Mex. 24N 105W
54 Durazno, Ur. 33S 57W
30 Durban, S. Afr. 30S 31E
49 Durham, N.C. 36N 79W
15 Durrës, Alb. 41N 19E
16 Dushanbe, Taj. 39N 69E
13 Düsseldorf, Ger. 51N 7E
11 Dzerzhinsk, Russia 56N 44E
16 Dzhambul, see Zhambyl, Kaz. 43N 71E

E

46 Eagle Pass, Tex. 29N 100W
36 East Chicago, Ind. 42N 87W
21 East China Sea, Asia 29N 124E
36 East Cleveland, Ohio 41N 82W
23 Eastern Ghāts (Mts.) India 16N 79E
37 East Hartford, Conn. 42N 73W
36 East Liverpool, Ohio 41N 81W
30 East London, S. Afr. 33S 28E
37 Easton, Pa. 41N 75W
37 East Orange, N.J. 41N 74W
37 East Providence, R.I. 42N 71W
45 East St. Louis, Ill. 39N 90W
14 Ebro (R.), Sp. 41N 0
28 Ech Cheliff, Alg. 36N 2E
14 Écija, Sp. 37N 5W
52 Ecuador (Ctry.) S.A. 1S 79W
15 Édhessa, Grc. 41N 22E
12 Edinburgh, Scot. 56N 3W
15 Edirne, Tur. 42N 27E
32 Edmonton, Alta., Can. 54N 114W
32 Edson, Alta., Can. 54N 117W
30 Edward, L., Ug.-Zaire 0 29E
29 Egypt (Ctry.) Afr. 27N 30E
13 Eisenach, Ger. 51N 10E
28 El Aaiún, W. Sah. 27N 13W
15 Elâziğ, Tur. 38N 39E
12 Elblag, Pol. 54N 19E
28 El Boulaïda, Alg. 37N 3E
11 El'brus, Gora (Mt.) Russia 43N 42E
22 Elburz Mts., Iran 37N 51E
28 El Djelfa, Alg. 35N 3E
45 El Dorado, Ark. 33N 93W
14 El Ferrol, Sp. 43N 8W
36 Elgin, Ill. 42N 88W
37 Elizabeth, N.J. 41N 74W
28 El Jadida, Mor. 33N 9W
28 El Kairouan, Tun. 36N 10E
36 Elkhart, Ind. 42N 86W
40 Elko, Nev. 41N 116W
40 Ellensburg, Wash. 47N 120W
36 Elmhurst, Ill. 42N 88W
37 Elmira, N.Y. 42N 77W
52 El Pao, Ven. 8N 63W
46 El Paso, Tex. 32N 106W
14 El Qala, Alg. 37N 8E
50 El Salvador (Ctry.) N.A. 14N 89W
23 Elūru, India 17N 80E
28 El Wad, Alg. 33N 7E
42 Ely, Nev. 39N 115W
36 Elyria, Ohio 41N 82W
22 Emāmshahr, Iran 36N 55E
45 Emporia, Kans. 38N 96W
11 Engel's, Russia 51N 46E
13 England (Polit. Reg.), U.K. 52N 2W
13 English Channel, Eur. 50N 2W
44 Enid, Okla. 36N 98W
13 Enschede, Neth. 52N 7E
50 Ensenada, Mex. 32N 116W
29 Entebbe, Ug. 0 32E
28 Enugu, Nig. 6N 7E
13 Épinal, Fr. 48N 6E
28 Equatorial Guinea (Ctry.) Afr. 3N 9E
15 Ereğli, Tur. 38N 34E
13 Erfurt, Ger. 51N 11E
37 Erie, Pa. 42N 80W
36 Erie, L., Can.-U.S. 42N 81W
29 Eritrea (Ctry.) Afr. 16N 38E
23 Ernākulam, India 10N 76E
12 Erne, L., N. Ire. 55N 8W
13 Erzgebirge (Ore Mts.), Ger.-Czech. 50N 13E

60 Lancaster, Ohio

36 Lancaster, Ohio 40N 83W
37 Lancaster, Pa. 40N 76W
24 Lang Son, Viet. 22N 107 E
20 Langzhong, China 32N 106 E
32 Lanigan, Sask., Can. 52N 105W
16 Länkäran, Azer 39N 49 E
36 Lansing, Mich. 43N 85W
20 Lanzhou, China 36N 104 E
24 Laoag, Phil. 18N 121 E
24 Laos (Ctry.) Asia 20N 102 E
52 La Paz, Bol. 17S 68W
50 La Paz, Mex. 24N 110W
12 Lapland (Reg.) Eur. 68N 25 E
54 La Plata, Arg. 35S 58W
17 Laptev Sea, Russia 75N 125 E
13 L'Aquila, It. 42N 13 E
28 Larache, Mor. 35N 6W
34 Laramie, Wyo. 41N 106W
46 Laredo, Tex. 28N 99W
54 La Rioja, Arg. 29S 67W
15 Lárisa, Grc. 40N 22 E
15 Larnaca, Cyp. 35N 34 E
31 Laas Caanood, Som. 8N 47 E
31 Laas Qoray, Som. 11N 48 E
43 Las Cruces, N. Mex. 32N 107W
54 La Serena, Chile 30S 71W
13 La Seyne, Fr. 43N 6 E
13 La Spezia, It. 44N 10 E
42 Las Vegas, Nev. 36N 115W
44 Las Vegas, N. Mex. 36N 105W
10 Latvia (Ctry.) Eur. 57N 25 E
27 Launceston, Austl. 42S 147 E
48 Laurel, Miss. 32N 89W
13 Lausanne, Switz. 47N 7 E
13 Laval, Fr. 48N 1W
45 Lawrence, Kans. 39N 95W
37 Lawrence, Mass. 43N 71W
44 Lawton, Okla. 35N 98W
38 Lead, S. Dak. 44N 104W
45 Leavenworth, Kans. 39N 95W
37 Lebanon, Pa. 40N 76W
15 Lebanon (Ctry.) Asia 34N 36 E
13 Lecce, It. 40N 18 E
12 Leeds, Eng. 54N 2W
13 Leeuwarden, Neth. 52N 6 E
25 Legazpi, Phil. 13N 124 E
13 Legnica, Pol. 51N 16 E
13 Le Havre, Fr. 50N 0
13 Leicester, Eng. 53N 1W
13 Leipzig, Ger. 51N 12 E
13 Le Mans, Fr. 48N 0
28 Lemdiyya, Alg. 36N 3 E
17 Lena (R.) Russia 72N 127 E
10 Leningrad, see St. Petersburg, Russia 60N 30 E
16 Leninogor, Kaz. 50N 83 E
37 Leominster, Mass. 43N 72W
50 León, Mex. 21N 102W
14 León, Sp. 43N 6W
13 Le Puy, Fr. 45N 4 E
14 Lérida, Sp. 42N 1 E
12 Lerwick, Scot. 60N 1W
20 Leshan, China 30N 104 E
30 Lesotho (Ctry.) Afr. 30S 28 E
51 Lesser Antilles (Is.) N.A.-S.A. 15N 61W
21 Lesser Khingan Range (Xiao Hinggan Ling), China 48N 128 E
24 Lesser Sunda Is., Indon. 9S 120 E
13 Leszno, Pol. 52N 17 E
40 Lewiston, Idaho 46N 117W
37 Lewiston, Maine 44N 70W
41 Lewistown, Mont. 47N 109W
36 Lexington, Ky. 38N 84W
20 Lhasa, China 30N 91 E
21 Liaoyang, China 41N 123 E
13 Liberec, Czech. 51N 15 E
28 Liberia (Ctry.) Afr. 6N 9W
30 Libreville, Gabon 0 9 E
29 Libya (Ctry.) Afr. 28N 18 E
29 Libyan Des., Afr. 28N 24 E
13 Liechtenstein (Ctry.) Eur. 47N 9 E
13 Liège, Bel. 51N 5 E
12 Liepāja, Lat. 57N 21 E
13 Ligurian Sea, Fr.-It. 43N 8 E
30 Likasi, Zaire 11S 27 E
13 Lille, Fr. 51N 3 E
36 Lima, Ohio 41N 84W
52 Lima, Peru 12S 77W
15 Limassol, Cyp. 35N 33 E
13 Limerick, Ire. 52N 9W
13 Limoges, Fr. 46N 1 E
30 Limpopo (R.) Afr. 23S 28 E
14 Linares, Sp. 38N 4W
13 Lincoln, Eng. 53N 1W
45 Lincoln, Nebr. 41N 97W
25 Lingayen, Phil. 16N 120 E
12 Linnköping, Swe. 58N 16 E
21 Linyi, China 35N 118 E
13 Linz, Aus. 48N 14 E
11 Lipetsk, Russia 52N 40 E
14 Lisbon, Port. 39N 9W
10 Lithuania (Ctry.) Eur. 56N 24W
30 Little Karroo (Plat.) S. Afr. 34S 21 E
45 Little Rock, Ark. 35N 92W
20 Liuzhou, China 24N 109 E
12 Liverpool, Eng. 53N 3W
41 Livingston, Mont. 46N 111W
30 Livingstone, Zambia 18S 26 E
15 Livno, Bos. 44N 17 E
13 Livorno, It. 44N 11 E
14 Ljubljana, Slo. 46N 14 E
13 Llanelli, Wales 52N 4W
52 Llanos (Reg.) Col.-Ven. 5N 70W
32 Lloydminster, Sask., Can. 53N 110W
30 Lobamba, Swaz 34N 32 E
30 Lobatse, Bots. 25S 26 E
37 Lockport, N.Y. 43N 79W
24 Loc Ninh, Viet. 12N 107 E
13 Łódź, Pol. 52N 19 E
41 Logan, Utah 42N 112W
32 Logan, Mt., Yukon, Can. 61N 141W
14 Logroño, Sp. 42N 2W
13 Loire (R.) Fr. 48N 2 E
54 Lomas de Zamora, Arg. 34S 58W
28 Lomé, Togo 6N 1 E
13 London, Eng. 51N 0
33 London, Ont., Can. 43N 82W
12 Londonderry, N. Ire. 55N 7W
54 Londrina, Braz. 23S 51W
42 Long Beach, Calif. 34N 118W
37 Long I., N.Y. 41N 73W
33 Long Range Mts., Newf., Can. 48N 57W
24 Long Xuyen, Viet. 11N 105 E
36 Lorain, Ohio 41N 82W
23 Loralai, Pak. 31N 69 E
14 Lorca, Sp. 38N 2W
13 Lorient, Fr. 48N 3W
43 Los Alamos, N. Mex. 36N 106W
42 Los Angeles, Calif. 34N 118W
54 Los Ángeles, Chile 37S 72W
53 Los Teques, Ven. 10N 67W
54 Lota, Chile 37S 73W
24 Louangphrabang, Laos 20N 102 E
35 Louisiana (State) U.S. 31N 92W
36 Louisville, Ky. 38N 86W
37 Lowell, Mass. 43N 71W
27 Lower Hutt, N.Z. 41S 175 E
15 Loznica, Yugo. 45N 19 E
30 Lualaba (R.) Zaire 10S 25 E
30 Luanda, Ang. 9S 13 E
44 Lubbock, Tex. 34N 102W
12 Lübeck, Ger. 54N 11 E
30 Lubilash (R.) Zaire 8S 24 E
13 Lublin, Pol. 51N 23 E
30 Lubumbashi (Elizabethville), Zaire 12S 28 E
13 Lucca, It. 44N 10 E
14 Lucena, Sp. 37N 4W
23 Lucknow, India 27N 81 E
23 Ludhiāna, India 31N 76 E
14 Lugo, Sp. 43N 8W
15 Lugoj, Rom. 46N 22 E
12 Luleå, Swe. 66N 22 E
20 Lun, Mong. 48N 105 E
12 Lund, Swe. 56N 13 E
21 Luoyang, China 35N 113 E
12 Lurgan, N. Ire. 54N 6W
30 Lusaka, Zambia 15S 28 E
21 Lüshun, China 39N 121 E
31 Luuq, Som. 10N 50 E
13 Luxembourg, Lux. 50N 6 E
13 Luxembourg (Ctry.) Eur. 50N 6 E
13 Luzern, Switz. 47N 8 E
20 Luzhou, China 29N 105 E
24 Luzon (I.) Phil. 17N 120 E
10 L'viv (Lvov), Ukr. 50N 24 E
37 Lynchburg, Va. 37N 79W
37 Lynn, Mass. 42N 71W
32 Lynn Lake, Man., Can. 57N 101W
13 Lyon, Fr. 46N 5 E
11 Lys'va, Russia 58N 58 E

M

21 Macao (Ctry.) Asia 22N 114 E
53 Macapá, Braz. 0 51W
26 Macdonnell Ranges, Austl. 24S 133 E
15 Macedonia (Ctry.) Eur. 42N 22 E
53 Maceió, Braz. 10S 36W
31 Macímboa da Praia, Moz. 11S 40 E
32 Mackenzie (R.) N.W. Ter., Can. 63N 124W
32 Mackenzie Mts., Can. 64N 130W
36 Mackinaw City, Mich. 46N 85W
48 Macon, Ga. 33N 84W
31 Madagascar (Ctry.) Afr. 20S 46 E
52 Madeira (R.) Bol.-Braz. 7S 63W
28 Madeira, Arquipélago da (Is.) Port. 33N 16W
39 Madison, Wis. 43N 89W
23 Madras, India 13N 80 E
50 Madre del Sur, Sierra (Mts.) Mex. 18N 101W
50 Madre Occidental, Sierra (Mts.) Mex. 23N 105W
50 Madre Oriental, Sierra (Mts.) Mex. 23N 100W
14 Madrid, Sp. 40N 4W
23 Madurai, India 10N 78 E
21 Maebashi, Japan 36N 139 E
30 Mafeking, S. Afr. 26S 25 E
17 Magadan, Russia 60N 151 E
54 Magallanes, Estrecho de (Str.) Arg.-Chile 53S 69W
52 Magdalena (R.) Col. 8N 74W
13 Magdeburg, Ger. 52N 12 E
53 Magé, Braz. 23S 43W
14 Maghniyya, Alg. 35N 2W
11 Magnitogorsk, Russia 53N 59 E
31 Mahajanga, Mad. 15S 46 E
14 Mahón, Sp. 40N 4 E
29 Maiduguri, Nig. 12N 13 E
27 Main Barrier Ra., Austl. 31S 142 E
30 Mai-Ndombe (L.) Zaire 2S 19 E
35 Maine (State) U.S. 45N 69W
13 Mainz, Ger. 50N 8 E
53 Maiquetía, Ven. 11N 67W
24 Makasar, Selat (Str.) Indon. 3S 118 E
30 Makgadikgadi Pans (Dry L.) Bots. 21S 26 E
11 Makiyivka, Ukr. 48N 38 E
16 Makushino, Russia 55N 68 E
28 Malabo, Eq. Gui. 4N 9 E
14 Málaga, Sp. 37N 4W
15 Malatya, Tur. 38N 38 E
30 Malawi (Ctry.) Afr. 11S 34 E
16 Malaya Vishera, Russia 59N 32 E
24 Malay Pen., Asia 8N 101 E
24 Malaysia (Ctry.) Asia 4N 102 E
12 Malbork, Pol. 54N 19 E
37 Malden, Mass. 42N 71W
9 Maldives (Ctry.), Ind. O. 5N 70 E
28 Mali (Ctry.) Afr. 16N 2W
15 Mallawī, Eg. 28N 31 E
14 Mallorca (I.) Sp. 40N 3 E
12 Malmö, Swe. 56N 13 E
14 Malta (Ctry.) Eur. 36N 14 E
25 Maluku (Moluccas) (Is.) Indon. 3S 127 E
25 Maluku, Laut (Molucca Sea), Indon. 0 125 E
25 Manado, Indon. 1N 125 E
50 Managua, Nic. 12N 86W
31 Manakara, Mad. 22S 48 E
20 Manas, China 44N 86 E
53 Manaus (Manaos), Braz. 3S 60W
37 Manchester, Conn. 42N 72W
12 Manchester, Eng. 53N 2W
37 Manchester, N.H. 43N 71W
21 Manchuria (Reg.) China 46N 126 E
20 Mandalay, Mya. 22N 96 E
38 Mandan, N. Dak. 47N 101W
22 Mandeb, Bab el (Str.) Afr.-Asia 13N 43 E
23 Māndvi, India 23N 69 E
23 Mangalore, India 13N 75 E
45 Manhattan, Kans. 39N 97W
25 Manila, Phil. 15N 121 E
15 Manisa, Tur. 39N 27 E
32 Manitoba (L.) Man., Can. 51N 99W
32 Manitoba (Prov.) Can. 55N 98W
39 Manitowoc, Wis. 44N 88W
52 Manizales, Col. 5N 76W
39 Mankato, Minn. 44N 94W
23 Mannar, G. of, India-Sri Lanka 9N 79 E
13 Mannheim, Ger. 49N 9 E
36 Mansfield, Ohio 41N 82W
51 Manzanillo, Cuba 20N 77W
21 Manzhouli, China 49N 117 E
30 Maputo, Moz. 26S 33 E
52 Maracaibo, Ven. 11N 72W
52 Maracaibo, Lago de (L.) Ven. 10N 72W
52 Maracay, Ven. 10N 68W
53 Marajó, Ilha de (I.) Braz. 1S 50W
52 Marañón (R.) Peru 5S 75W
54 Mar del Plata, Arg. 38S 58W
22 Mardin, Tur. 37N 41 E
51 Marianao, Cuba 23N 82W
15 Maribor, Slo. 47N 16 E
53 Marilia, Braz. 23S 50W
36 Marion, Ind. 41N 86W
36 Marion, Ohio 41N 83W
11 Mariupol', Ukr. 47N 38W
25 Mariveles, Phil. 14N 120 E
31 Marka, Som. 2N 45 E
17 Markovo, Russia 65N 170 E
15 Marmara Denizi (Sea) Tur. 41N 28 E
29 Maroua, Cam. 11N 14 E
39 Marquette, Mich. 46N 88W
28 Marrakech, Mor. 32N 8W
13 Marsala, It. 38N 12 E
13 Marseille, Fr. 43N 5 E
47 Marshall, Tex. 33N 94W
9 Marshall Is. (Ctry.), Pac. O. 10N 170 E
37 Martha's Vineyard (I.) Mass. 41N 70W
51 Martinique (Ctry.) N.A. 15N 61W
32 Martre, Lac la (L.) N.W. Ter., Can. 64N 120W
16 Mary, Turk. 38N 62 E
35 Maryland (State) U.S. 39N 76W
21 Masan, Kor. 35N 129 E
30 Maseru, Leso. 29S 27 E
22 Mashhad, Iran 36N 59 E
22 Masjed Soleymān, Iran 32N 49 E
39 Mason City, Iowa 43N 93W
35 Massachusetts (State) U.S. 42N 72W
32 Masset, B.C., Can. 54N 132W
36 Massillon, Ohio 41N 82W
30 Matadi, Zaire 6S 14 E
50 Matamoros, Mex. 26N 97W
51 Matanzas, Cuba 23N 82W
23 Matara, Sri Lanka 6N 81 E
24 Mataram, Indon. 9S 116 E
23 Mathura, India 28N 78 E
16 Matochkin Shar, Russia 74N 56 E
22 Maṭraḥ, Oman 24N 58 E
21 Matsue, Japan 35N 133 E
21 Matsuyama, Japan 34N 133 E
52 Maturin, Ven. 10N 63W
30 Maun, Bots. 20S 24 E
28 Mauritania (Ctry.) Afr. 19N 12W
9 Mauritius (Ctry.), Afr. 20S 58 E
24 Mawlamyine, Mya. 16N 98 E
51 Mayagüez, P.R. 18N 67W
11 Maykop, Russia 45N 40 E
32 Mayo, Yukon, Can. 64N 136W
50 Mayran, Laguna de (L.) Mex. 26N 103W
23 Mazār-e Sharīf, Afg. 37N 67 E
50 Mazatlán, Mex. 23N 106W
30 Mbabane, Swaz. 26S 31 E
30 Mbandaka, Zaire 0 18 E
30 M'banza Congo, Ang. 7S 14 E
45 McAlester, Okla. 35N 96W
46 McAllen, Tex. 26N 98W
34 McGrath, Alsk. 63N 155W
37 McKeesport, Pa. 40N 80W
34 McKinley, Mt., Alsk. 63N 150W
32 McLennan, Alta., Can. 56N 117W
22 Mecca (Makkah), Sau. Ar. 21N 40 E
24 Medan, Indon. 4N 99 E
52 Medellín, Col. 6N 76W
40 Medford, Oreg. 42N 123W
14 Mediterranean Sea, Afr.-Asia-Eur. 38N 10 E
16 Mednogorsk, Russia 51N 57 E
23 Meerut, India 29N 78 E
28 Meknès, Mor. 34N 6W
24 Mekong (R.) Asia 18N 104 E
24 Melaka, Mala. 2N 102 E
27 Melbourne, Austl. 38S 145 E
32 Melfort, Sask., Can. 53N 105W
14 Melilla, Afr. 35N 3W
11 Melitopol', Ukr. 47N 35 E
32 Melville, Sask., Can. 51N 103W
33 Melville Pen., N.W. Ter., Can. 68N 85W
48 Memphis, Tenn. 35N 90W
54 Mendoza, Arg. 33S 69W
14 Menorca (I.) Sp. 40N 4 E
14 Menzel Bourguiba, Tun. 37N 10 E
13 Merano, It. 46N 11 E
25 Merauke, Pap. N. Gui. 9S 140 E
54 Mercedario, C. (Mt.) Arg.-Chile 32S 70W
54 Mercedes, Arg. 29S 58W
24 Mergui, Bur. 12N 99 E
50 Mérida, Mex. 21N 90W
52 Mérida, Ven. 8N 71W
37 Meriden, Conn. 41N 73W
48 Meridian, Miss. 32N 89W
13 Messina, It. 38N 16 E
47 Metairie, La. 30N 90W
12 Metz, Fr. 49N 6 E
50 Mexicali, Mex. 32N 115W
50 Mexico (Ctry.) N.A. 24N 102W
50 Mexico, G. of,, N.A. 25N 90W
50 Mexico City, Mex. 19N 99W
11 Mezen', Russia 66N 44 E
43 Miami, Ariz. 33N 111W
49 Miami, Fla. 26N 80W
49 Miami Beach, Fla. 26N 80W
35 Michigan (State) U.S. 44N 85W
36 Michigan City, Ind. 42N 87W
36 Michigan, L.,, U.S. 44N 87W
33 Michikamau (L.) Newf., Can. 54N 63W
11 Michurinsk, Russia 53N 41 E
9 Micronesia, Federated States of (Ctry.), Pac. O. 5N 153 E
12 Middlesbrough, Eng. 55N 1W
37 Middletown, Conn. 42N 73W
36 Middletown, Ohio 39N 84W
46 Midland, Tex. 32N 102W
8 Midway Is. (Ctry.), Pac. O. 30N 175W
13 Milan, It. 45N 9 E
41 Miles City, Mont. 46N 106W
39 Milwaukee, Wis. 43N 88W
54 Minas, Ur. 34S 55W
50 Minatitlán, Mex. 18N 95W
25 Mindanao (I.) Phil. 8N 125 E
25 Mindoro (I.) Phil. 13N 120 E
39 Minneapolis, Minn. 45N 93W
32 Minnedosa, Man., Can. 50N 100W
38 Minnesota (R.) Minn. 45N 96W
35 Minnesota (State) U.S. 46N 95W
38 Minot, N. Dak. 48N 101W
10 Minsk, Bela. 54N 28 E
17 Minusinsk, Russia 54N 92 E
53 Miracema do Tocantins, Braz. 9S 48W
22 Mirbāṭ, Oman 17N 55 E
54 Mirim, L., Braz. 33S 54W
23 Mirzāpur, India 25N 83 E
36 Mishawaka, Ind. 42N 86W
13 Miskolc, Hung. 48N 21 E
29 Misrātah, Libya 32N 15 E
35 Mississippi (R.) U.S. 32N 92W
35 Mississippi (State) U.S. 33N 90W
41 Missoula, Mont. 47N 114W
35 Missouri (R.) U.S. 41N 96W
35 Missouri (State) U.S. 38N 93W
52 Misti, Volcán (Vol.) Peru 16S 71W
38 Mitchell, S. Dak. 44N 98W
15 Mitilíni, Grc. 39N 27 E
29 Mitsiwa, Erit. 16N 39 E
30 Mmabatho, Bophuthatswana 26S 26 E
45 Moberly, Mo. 39N 92W
48 Mobile, Ala. 31N 88W
13 Modena, It. 45N 11 E
31 Mogadishu, Som. 2N 45 E
54 Mogi das Cruzes, Braz. 24S 46W
10 Mogilev, Bela. 54N 30 E
15 Mohyliv-Podil's'kyy, Ukr. 48N 28 E
15 Moldova (Ctry.) Eur. 47N 29 E
13 Molfetta, It. 41N 17 E
39 Moline, Ill. 42N 90W
31 Mombasa, Ken. 4S 40 E
13 Monaco (Ctry.) Eur. 44N 8 E
14 Monastir, Tun. 36N 11 E
33 Moncton, N.B., Can. 46N 65W
23 Monghyr, India 25N 87 E
20 Mongolia (Ctry.) Asia 46N 100 E
47 Monroe, La. 32N 92W
36 Monroe, Mich. 42N 83W
28 Monrovia, Lib. 6N 11W
13 Mons, Bel. 50N 4 E
34 Montana (State) U.S. 47N 109W
13 Montauban, Fr. 44N 1 E
51 Montego Bay, Jam. 18N 78W

Pereira, Col. **61**

15 Montenegro (Rep.) Yugo. 43N 19 E
42 Monterey, Calif. 37N 122W
52 Montería, Col. 9N 76W
50 Monterrey, Mex. 26N 100W
13 Monte Sant'Angelo, It. . . . 42N 16 E
54 Montevideo, Ur. 35S 56W
48 Montgomery, Ala. 32N 86W
13 Montluçon, Fr. . . . . 46N 3 E
37 Montpelier, Vt. 44N 73W
13 Montpellier, Fr. . . . . 44N 4 E
33 Montréal, Que., Can. 45N 74W
51 Montserrat (Ctry.) N.A. . . . 17N 63W
20 Monywa, Mya. . . . . 22N 95 E
32 Moose Jaw, Sask., Can. . . . 50N 106W
33 Moosonee, Ont., Can. 51N 81W
23 Morādābād, India 29N 79W
32 Morden, Man., Can. 49N 98W
50 Morelia, Mex. 20N 101W
14 Morena, Sa. (Mts.) Sp. . . . 38N 6W
47 Morgan City, La. 30N 91W
21 Morioka, Japan . . . . 40N 141 E
13 Morlaix, Fr. 49N 4W
28 Morocco (Ctry.) Afr. 32N 6W
31 Morombe, Mad. . . . . 22S 44 E
54 Morón, Arg. 34S 59W
32 Morris, Man., Can. 49N 98W
11 Morshansk, Russia . . . . . . 53N 42 E
40 Moscow, Idaho 47N 117W
11 Moscow (Moskva), Russia 56N 38 E
51 Mosquitos, Golfo de los (G.) Pan. 9N 81W
15 Mostar, Bos. . . . . 43N 18 E
12 Motherwell, Scot. 56N 4W
28 Mouaskar, Alg. 35N 0
13 Moulins, Fr. . . . . 47N 3 E
36 Mount Carmel, Ill. 38N 88W
37 Mount Vernon, N.Y. 41N 74W
30 Mozambique (Ctry.) Afr. 18S 35 E
31 Mozambique Chan., Afr. 20S 40 E
15 Mukacheve, Ukr. . . . . 48N 23 E
17 Mukhtuya, Russia . . . . 61N 113 E
13 Mulhouse, Fr. . . . . 48N 7 E
23 Multān, Pak. . . . . 30N 71 E
36 Muncie, Ind. 40N 85W
13 Munich (München), Ger. 48N 12 E
13 Münster, Ger. . . . . 52N 8 E
14 Murcia, Sp. 38N 1W
10 Murmansk, Russia . . . . . . 69N 33 E
16 Murom, Russia . . . . 55N 42 E
21 Muroran, Japan . . . . 42N 141 E
26 Murray Bridge, Austl. . . . . 35S 140 E
22 Muscat, Oman . . . . 23N 58 E
36 Muskegon, Mich. 43N 86W
45 Muskogee, Okla. 36N 95W
20 Myanmar (Ctry.), Asia . . . 22N 95 E
20 Myitkyina, Mya. . . . . 26N 97 E
11 Mykolayiv, Ukr. . . . . 47N 32 E
23 Mymensingh, Bngl. . . . . . . 25N 90 E
23 Mysore, India . . . . 13N 77 E

N

11 Naberezhnyye Chelny, Russia . . . . 56N 52 E
28 Nabeul, Tun. . . . . 37N 11 E
15 Nabulus, Jor. . . . . 32N 35 E
31 Nacala, Moz. . . . . 15S 41 E
12 Naestved, Den. . . . . 55N 12 E
25 Naga, Phil. . . . . 14N 123 E
21 Nagano, Japan . . . . 37N 138 E
21 Nagaoka, Japan . . . . 37N 139 E
23 Nāgappattinam, India . . . . 11N 80 E
21 Nagasaki, Japan . . . . 33N 130 E
21 Nagoya, Japan . . . . 35N 137 E
23 Nāgpur, India . . . . 21N 79 E
13 Nagykanizsa, Hung. . . . . . 46N 17 E
21 Naha, Japan . . . . 26N 128 E
52 Naiguatá, Ven. 11N 67W
31 Nairobi, Ken. . . . . 1S 37 E
21 Najin, Kor. . . . . 42N 130 E
17 Nakhodka, Russia . . . . 43N 133 E
24 Nakhon Ratchasima, Thai. 15N 102 E
12 Nakskov, Den. . . . . 55N 11 E
23 Namangan, Uzb. . . . . 41N 72 E
20 Nam Co (L.) China . . . . . . 31N 91 E
24 Nam Dinh, Viet. . . . . 20N 106 E
30 Namib Des., Nam. . . . . . . 24S 15 E
30 Namibia (Ctry.) Afr. . . . . 21S 16 E
40 Nampa, Idaho 44N 117W
21 Namp'o, Kor. . . . . 39N 125 E
13 Namur, Bel. . . . . 50N 5 E
21 Nanchang, China . . . . 29N 116 E
20 Nanchong, China . . . . 31N 106 E
13 Nancy, Fr. . . . . 49N 6 E
23 Nanda-Devi (Mt.) India . . . 30N 80 E
21 Nanjing, China . . . . 32N 119 E
20 Nanning, China . . . . 23N 108 E
21 Nanping, China . . . . 26N 118 E
21 Nansei Shotō (Is.) Japan 28N 128 E
13 Nantes, Fr. 47N 2W
21 Nanyang, China . . . . 33N 113 E
42 Napa, Calif. 38N 122W
13 Naples, It. . . . . 41N 14 E
21 Nara, Japan . . . . 35N 136 E
13 Narbonne, Fr. . . . . 43N 3 E
12 Narvik, Nor. . . . . 68N 17 E
11 Nar'yan-Mar, Russia . . . . . 68N 53 E
16 Narym, Russia . . . . 59N 82 E
16 Naryn, Kyrg. . . . . 41N 76 E
37 Nashua, N.H. 43N 71W
48 Nashville, Tenn. 36N 87W
15 Našice, Cro. . . . . 45N 18 E
23 Nāsik, India . . . . 20N 74 E
51 Nassau, Bahamas 25N 77W
53 Natal, Braz. 6S 35W
48 Natchez, Miss. 32N 91W
9 Nauru (Ctry.), Pac. O. . . . . 3S 170 E
15 Nazareth, Isr. . . . . 33N 35 E
29 N'Djamena, Chad . . . . 12N 15 E
30 Ndola, Zambia . . . . 13S 29 E
12 Neagh, L., N. Ire. 55N 7W
22 Nebit-Dag, Turk. . . . . 39N 54 E
34 Nebraska (State) U.S. 42N 101W
32 Neepawa, Man., Can. 50N 100W
52 Negro (R.), S.A. 0 64W
52 Neiva, Col. 3N 75W
32 Nelson, B.C., Can. 49N 117W
32 Nelson (R.) Can. 56N 94W
23 Nepal (Ctry.) Asia . . . . 28N 84 E
17 Nerchinsk, Russia . . . . 52N 116 E
13 Netherlands (Ctry.) Eur. 53N 5 E
13 Neuchâtel, Switz. . . . . 47N 7 E
12 Neumünster, Ger. . . . . 54N 10 E
54 Neuquén, Arg. 39S 68W
13 Neusiedler See (L.) Aus.-Hung. . . . . 48N 16 E
34 Nevada (State) U.S. 39N 117W
14 Nevada, Sa. (Mts.) Sp. 37N 3W
13 Nevers, Fr. . . . . 47N 3 E
16 Nev'yansk, Russia . . . . 57N 60 E
36 New Albany, Ind. 38N 86W
37 Newark, N.J. 41N 73W
36 Newark, Ohio 40N 82W
37 New Bedford, Mass. 42N 71W
49 New Bern, N.C. 35N 77W
37 New Britain, Conn. 42N 73W
37 New Brunswick, N.J. 40N 74W
33 New Brunswick (Prov.) Can. 47N 66W
27 New Caledonia (Ctry.) Pac. O. . . . . 21S 164 E
27 Newcastle, Austl. . . . . 33S 152 E
37 New Castle, Pa. 41N 80W
12 Newcastle upon Tyne, Eng. 55N 2W
23 New Delhi, India . . . . 29N 77 E
33 Newfoundland (Prov.) Can. 48N 56W
25 New Guinea (I.) Asia-Oc. . 5S 140 E
35 New Hampshire (State) U.S. 44N 72W
37 New Haven, Conn. 41N 73W
35 New Jersey (State) U.S. . . . 40N 74W
37 New London, Conn. 41N 72W
34 New Mexico (State) U.S. 35N 108W
47 New Orleans, La. 30N 90W
13 Newport, Eng. 51N 1W
37 Newport, R.I. 41N 71W
37 Newport News, Va. 37N 76W
37 Newton, Mass. 42N 71W
37 New York, N.Y. 41N 74W
35 New York (State) U.S. 43N 76W
27 New Zealand (Ctry.) Pac. O. . . . . 39S 170 E
22 Neyshābūr, Iran . . . . 36N 59 E
24 Nha Trang, Viet. . . . . 12N 109 E
37 Niagara Falls, N.Y. 43N 79W
28 Niamey, Niger . . . . 14N 2 E
50 Nicaragua (Ctry.) N.A. . . . 13N 86W
13 Nicastro, It. . . . . 39N 16 E
13 Nice, Fr. . . . . 44N 7 E
24 Nicobar Is., India . . . . 8N 94 E
15 Nicosia, Cyp. . . . . 35N 33 E
15 Niğde, Tur. . . . . 38N 35 E
28 Niger (Ctry.) Afr. . . . . 16N 8 E
28 Niger (R.) Afr. . . . . 8N 6 E
28 Nigeria (Ctry.) Afr. . . . . . . 9N 8 E
21 Niigata, Japan . . . . 38N 139 E
11 Nikolayev, see Mykolayiv, Ukr. . . . . 47N 32 E
16 Nikol'sk, Russia . . . . 59N 46 E
15 Nikopol, Bul. . . . . 44N 25 E
11 Nikopol', Ukr. . . . . 48N 34 E
29 Nile (R.) Eg.-Sud. . . . . 28N 30 E
54 Nilópolis, Braz. 23S 43W
13 Nîmes, Fr. . . . . 44N 4 E
22 Nineveh (Ruins) Iraq . . . . 36N 43 E
21 Ningbo, China . . . . 30N 121 E
21 Ningde, China . . . . 26N 120 E
33 Nipigon, Ont., Can. 49N 88W
33 Nipigon (L.) Ont., Can. . . . 50N 89W
15 Niš, Yugo. . . . . 43N 22 E
54 Niterói, Braz. 23S 43W
17 Nizhne-Angarsk, Russia . . . 56N 109 E
17 Nizhne-Kolymsk, Russia 69N 161 E
11 Nizhniy Novgorod, Russia 56N 44 E
11 Nizhniy Tagil, Russia . . . 58N 60 E
17 Nizhnyaya Tunguska (R.) Russia . . . . 64N 92 E
11 Nizhyn, Ukr. . . . . 51N 32 E
23 Noākhāli, Bngl. . . . . 23N 91 E
23 Noākhāli, Bngl. . . . . 23N 91 E
31 Nogai Valley, Som. . . . . . . 8N 48 E
43 Nogales, Ariz. 31N 111W
50 Nogales, Mex. 31N 111W
11 Noginsk, Russia . . . . 56N 38 E
34 Nome, Alsk. 64N 165W
17 Nordvik, Russia . . . . 74N 111 E
38 Norfolk, Nebr. 42N 97W
37 Norfolk, Va. 37N 76W
17 Noril'sk, Russia . . . . 69N 87 E
37 Norristown, Pa. 40N 75W
12 Norrköping, Swe. . . . . 59N 16 E
13 Northampton, Eng. 52N 1W
37 Northampton, Mass. 42N 73W
35 North Carolina (State) U.S. 36N 79W
36 North Channel (B.) Can. 46N 83W
36 North Chicago, Ill. 42N 88W
34 North Dakota (State) U.S. 48N 100W
12 Northern Ireland (Polit. Reg.), U.K. 55N 7W
9 Northern Mariana Is. (Ctry.), Pac. O. . . . . . . 16N 146 E
50 North Gamboa, Pan. 9N 80W
27 North I., N.Z. . . . . 38S 171 E
36 North Judson, Ind. 41N 87W
45 North Little Rock, Ark. . . . 35N 92W
44 North Platte (R.) Nebr. . . . 41N 101W
32 North Saskatchewan (R.) Can. 54N 111W
12 North Sea, Eur. . . . . 56N 2 E
37 North Tonawanda, N.Y. 43N 79W
32 North Vancouver, B.C., Can. 49N 105W
32 Northwest Territories, Can. 65N 105W
37 Norwalk, Conn. 41N 73W
12 Norway (Ctry.) Eur. . . . . . 65N 13 E
12 Norwegian Sea, Eur. . . . . . 66N 1 E
37 Norwich, Conn. 41N 72W
13 Norwich, Eng. . . . . 53N 1 E
36 Norwood, Ohio 39N 84W
13 Nottingham, Eng. 53N 1W
28 Nouakchott, Maur. 18N 16W
27 Noumea, N. Cal. . . . . 22S 167 E
54 Nova Iguaçu, Braz. 23S 43W
30 Nova Mambone, Moz. . . . 21S 35 E
13 Novara, It. . . . . 45N 9 E
33 Nova Scotia (Prov.) Can. 45N 64W
16 Novaya Zemlya (Is.) Russia . . . . 72N 54 E
13 Nové Zámky, Slov. . . . . . . 48N 18 E
10 Novgorod, Russia . . . . 59N 31 E
15 Novi-Pazar, Yugo. . . . . . . 43N 20 E
15 Novi Sad, Yugo. . . . . 45N 20 E
11 Novocherkassk, Russia . . . 47N 40 E
16 Novokuznetsk, Russia . . . . 54N 87 E
11 Novomoskovsk, Russia . . . 54N 38 E
11 Novorossiysk, Russia . . . . 45N 38 E
16 Novosibirsk, Russia . . . . . 55N 83 E
17 Novosibirskiye Ostrava (New Siberian Is.), Russia . . . . 75N 141 E
16 Novyy Port, Russia . . . . . . 67N 72 E
13 Nowy Sącz, Pol. . . . . 50N 21 E
30 Ntwetwe Pan (Basin) Bots. 20S 25 E
29 Nubian Des., Sud. . . . . . . 21N 33 E
50 Nuevo Laredo, Mex. 27N 99W
50 Nuevo San Juan, Pan. 9N 80W
26 Nullarbor Plain, Austl. . . . 32S 128 E
16 Nurata, Uzb. . . . . 41N 65 E
13 Nürnberg, Ger. . . . . 49N 11 E
23 Nushki, Pak. . . . . 29N 66 E
29 Nyala, Sud. . . . . 12N 25 E
30 Nyasa, L., Afr. . . . . 12S 35 E
13 Nyíregyháza, Hung. . . . . . 48N 22 E

O

42 Oakland, Calif. 38N 122W
36 Oak Park, Ill. 42N 88W
48 Oak Ridge, Tenn. 36N 84W
50 Oaxaca, Mex. 17N 97W
16 Ob' (R.) Russia . . . . 63N 67 E
52 Occidental, Cordillera (Ra.) Peru 10S 77W
15 Ödemiş, Tur. . . . . 38N 28 E
12 Odense, Den. . . . . 55N 10 E
11 Odesa (Odessa), Ukr. . . . . 46N 31 E
28 Ogbomosho, Nig. . . . . 8N 4 E
41 Ogden, Utah 41N 112W
32 Ogilvie Mts., Yukon, Can. 65N 139W
36 Ohio (R.) U.S. 37N 88W
35 Ohio (State) U.S. 40N 83W
21 Okayama, Japan . . . . 35N 134 E
17 Okha, Russia . . . . 54N 143 E
17 Okhotsk, Sea of, Japan-Russia . . . . 57N 147 E
34 Oklahoma (State) U.S. . . . 36N 98W
45 Oklahoma City, Okla. 35N 98W
30 Okovango Swamp, Bots. 19S 23 E
54 Olavarría, Arg. 37S 60W
32 Old Crow, Yukon, Can. . . . 68N 140W
13 Oldenburg, Ger. . . . . 53N 8 E
32 Olds, Alta., Can. 52N 114W
37 Olean, N.Y. 42N 78W
17 Olekminsk, Russia . . . . . . 61N 121 E
17 Ol'ga, Russia . . . . 44N 136 E
14 Olhão, Port. 37N 8W
53 Olinda, Braz. 8S 35W
54 Olivos, Arg. 34S 58W
13 Olomouc, Czech. . . . . 50N 17 E
14 Olot, Sp. . . . . 42N 3 E
12 Olsztyn, Pol. . . . . 54N 20 E
40 Olympia, Wash. 47N 123W
45 Omaha, Nebr. 41N 96W
22 Oman (Ctry.) Asia . . . . . . 19N 57 E
22 Oman, G. of, Asia . . . . . . 25N 57 E
29 Omdurman, Sud. . . . . 16N 32 E
16 Omsk, Russia . . . . 55N 73 E
21 Öndörhaan, Mong. . . . . . . 47N 111 E
11 Onega, Russia . . . . 64N 38 E
11 Onezhskoye Ozero (L. Onega), Russia . . . . 62N 37 E
28 Onitsha, Nig. . . . . 6N 6 E
33 Ontario (Prov.) Can. 50N 89W
37 Ontario, L., Can.-U.S. 44N 78W
13 Oostende, Bel. . . . . 51N 3 E
13 Opole, Pol. . . . . 51N 18 E
15 Oradea, Rom. . . . . 47N 22 E
11 Oral, Kaz. . . . . 51N 51 E
28 Oran, Alg. 36N 1W
30 Orange (R.) Afr. . . . . 29S 18 E
30 Oranjemund, Nam. . . . . . . 29S 16 E
15 Ordu, Tur. . . . . 41N 38 E
12 Örebro, Swe. . . . . 59N 15 E
34 Oregon (State) U.S. 44N 120W
16 Orekhovo-Zuyevo, Russia 56N 39 E
11 Orël, Russia . . . . 53N 36 E
11 Orenburg, Russia . . . . 52N 55 E
52 Oriental, Cordillera (Ra.) S.A. 14S 68W
52 Orinoco (R.) Col.-Ven. 8N 65W
13 Oristano, It. . . . . 40N 9 E
50 Orizaba, Mex. 19N 97W
12 Orkney Is., Scot. 59N 2W
49 Orlando, Fla. 29N 81W
13 Orléans, Fr. . . . . 48N 2 E
11 Orsk, Russia . . . . 51N 59 E
52 Oruro, Bol. 18S 67W
21 Ōsaka, Japan . . . . 35N 135 E
16 Osh, Kyrg. . . . . 40N 73 E
33 Oshawa, Ont., Can. 44N 79W
39 Oshkosh, Wis. 44N 89W
28 Oshogbo, Nig. . . . . 8N 4 E
15 Osijek, Cro. . . . . 46N 19 E
12 Oslo, Nor. 60N 11W
54 Osorno, Chile 41S 73W
13 Ostrava, Czech. . . . . 50N 18 E
13 Ostrowiec Świętokrzyski, Pol. . . . . 51N 21 E
13 Ostrów Wielkopolski, Pol. 52N 18 E
21 Otaru, Japan . . . . 43N 141 E
33 Ottawa, Ont., Can. 45N 76W
33 Ottawa (R.) Can. 46N 77W
39 Ottumwa, Iowa 41N 92W
28 Ouagadougou, Burkina . . . 12N 2W
28 Oujda, Mor. 35N 2W
12 Oulu, Fin. . . . . 65N 26 E
33 Outardes, R. aux (R.) Que., Can. 52N 70W
14 Oviedo, Sp. 43N 6W
36 Owensboro, Ky. 38N 87W
13 Oxford, Eng. 52N 1W
36 Oxford, Ohio 39N 85W
28 Oyo, Nig. . . . . 8N 4 E
13 Ozieri, It. . . . . 41N 9 E

P

50 Pachuca, Mex. 20N 99W
8 Pacific Ocean 10S 150W
24 Padang, Indon. . . . . 1S 100 E
13 Padova, It. . . . . 45N 12 E
47 Padre I., Tex. 27N 97W
12 Paisley, Scot. 56N 4W
23 Pakistan (Ctry.) Asia . . . . 30N 71 E
20 Pakokku, Mya. . . . . 21N 95 E
17 Palana, Russia . . . . 59N 160 E
9 Palau (Ctry.), Pac. O. . . . . 8N 135 E
24 Palembang, Indon. . . . . . . 3S 105 E
14 Palencia, Sp. 42N 5W
13 Palermo, It. . . . . 38N 13 E
19 Palestine (Reg.) Asia . . . . 32N 35 E
14 Palma, Sp. . . . . 40N 3 E
52 Palmira, Col. 4N 76W
52 Palúa, Ven. 9N 63W
22 Pamirs (Mts.) Asia . . . . . . 38N 73 E
44 Pampa, Tex. 36N 101W
54 Pampa (Reg.) Arg. 35S 64W
23 Panaji (Panjim), India . . . . 16N 74 E
51 Panamá, Pan. 9N 80W
51 Panama (Ctry.) N.A. 8N 80W
51 Panama, G. of, Pan. 8N 80W
48 Panama City, Fla. 30N 86W
15 Pančevo, Yugo. . . . . 45N 21 E
13 Pápa, Hung. . . . . 47N 17 E
25 Papua New Guinea (Ctry.) Pac. O. . . . . 7S 142 E
54 Paraguay (R.) S.A. 25S 58W
54 Paraguay (Ctry.) S.A. 24S 57W
53 Paramaribo, Sur. 5N 55W
54 Paraná, Arg. 32S 60W
54 Paraná (R.) S.A. 25S 54W
13 Paris, Fr. . . . . 49N 2 E
45 Paris, Tex. 34N 96W
36 Parkersburg, W. Va. 39N 82W
13 Parma, It. . . . . 45N 10 E
36 Parma, Ohio 41N 82W
53 Parnaíba, Braz. 3S 42W
12 Pärnu, Est. . . . . 58N 24 E
45 Parsons, Kans. 37N 95W
42 Pasadena, Calif. 34N 118W
37 Passaic, N.J. 41N 74W
52 Pasto, Col. 1N 77W
54 Patagonia (Reg.) Arg. 44S 46W
24 Pathein, Mya. . . . . 17N 95 E
23 Patiāla, India . . . . 30N 76 E
23 Patna, India . . . . 26N 85 E
54 Patos, Lago dos (L.) Braz. 31S 53W
15 Pátrai, Grc. . . . . 38N 22 E
37 Patterson, N.J. 41N 74W
13 Pau, Fr. 43N 0
13 Pavia, It. . . . . 45N 9 E
16 Pavlodar, Kaz. . . . . 52N 77 E
15 Pavlohrad, Ukr. . . . . 49N 36 E
37 Pawtucket, R.I. 42N 71W
54 Paysandú, Ur. 32S 58W
37 Peabody, Mass. 43N 71W
32 Peace (R.) Can. 57N 117W
31 Pebane, Moz. . . . . 17S 38 E
13 Peć, Yugo. . . . . 43N 20 E
10 Pechenga, Russia . . . . 70N 31 E
34 Pecos (R.) U.S. 31N 103W
15 Pećs, Hung. . . . . 46N 18 E
17 Peleduy, Russia . . . . 60N 113 E
32 Pelly Mts., Yukon, Can. 62N 134W
54 Pelotas, Braz. 32S 52W
33 Pembroke, Ont., Can. 46N 77W
40 Pendleton, Oreg. 46N 119W
35 Pennsylvania (State) U.S. 41N 78W
48 Pensacola, Fla. 30N 87W
32 Penticton, B.C., Can. 49N 119W
11 Penza, Russia . . . . 53N 45 E
17 Penzhino, Russia . . . . 64N 168 E
36 Peoria, Ill. 41N 90W
52 Pereira, Col. 5N 76W

62 *Pergamino, Arg.*

54 Pergamino, Arg. 34S 61W
13 Perigueux, Fr. 45N 1E
11 Perm', Russia 58N 56E
15 Pernik, Bul. 43N 23E
13 Perpignan, Fr. 43N 3E
22 Persian G., Asia 28N 50E
26 Perth, Austl. 32S 116E
12 Perth, Scot. 56N 3W
37 Perth Amboy, N.J. 41N 74W
52 Peru (Ctry.) S.A. 10S 75W
13 Perugia, It. 43N 12E
15 Pervomays'k, Ukr. 48N 31E
13 Pesaro, It. 44N 13E
23 Peshāwar, Pak. 34N 72E
33 Peterborough, Ont., Can. 44N 78W
49 Petersburg, Va. 37N 78W
15 Petrich, Bul. 41N 23E
16 Petropavl, Kaz. 55N 69E
17 Petropavlovsk-Kamchatskiy, Russia 53N 159E
54 Petrópolis, Braz. 23S 43W
11 Petrozavodsk, Russia 62N 34E
48 Phenix City, Ala. 32N 85W
37 Philadelphia, Pa. 40N 75W
25 Philippines (Ctry.) Asia 14N 125E
21 Philippine Sea, Asia 25N 129E
24 Phitsanulok, Thai. 17N 100E
24 Phnum Pénh, Camb. 12N 105E
43 Phoenix, Ariz. 33N 112W
24 Phra Nakhon Si Ayutthaya, Thai. 14N 101E
13 Piacenza, It. 45N 10E
15 Piatra-Neamt, Rom. 47N 26E
50 Piedras Negras, Mex. 29N 101W
38 Pierre, S. Dak. 44N 100W
30 Pietermaritzburg, S. Afr. 30S 30E
14 Pieve, It. 46N 12E
54 Pilcomayo (R.) S.A. 24S 60W
51 Pinar del Río, Cuba 22N 84W
45 Pine Bluff, Ark. 34N 92W
16 Pinega, Russia 65N 43E
10 Pinsk, Bela. 52N 26E
13 Piombino, It. 43N 11E
13 Piotrkow Trybunalski, Pol. 51N 20E
53 Piracicaba, Braz. 23S 48W
15 Piraiévs, Grc. 38N 24E
15 Pirot, Yugo. 43N 23E
13 Pisa, It. 44N 10E
13 Pistoia, It. 44N 12E
8 Pitcairn (Ctry.), Pac. O. 25S 120W
15 Pitesti, Rom. 45N 25E
45 Pittsburg, Kans. 37N 95W
37 Pittsburgh, Pa. 40N 80W
37 Pittsfield, Mass. 42N 73W
52 Piura, Peru 5S 81W
37 Plainfield, N.J. 41N 74W
54 Plata, R. de la, Arg.-Ur. 35S 58W
38 Platte (R.) Nebr. 41N 100W
13 Plauen, Ger. 50N 12E
15 Pleven, Bul. 43N 24E
15 Pljevlja, Yugo. 43N 19E
15 Ploieşti, Rom. 45N 26E
15 Plovdiv, Bul. 42N 25E
13 Plymouth, Eng. 50N 4W
13 Plzeň, Czech. 50N 13E
13 Po (R.) It. 45N 11E
41 Pocatello, Idaho 43N 112W
51 Pointe-à-Pitre, Guad. 16N 62W
30 Pointe Noire, Congo 5S 12E
13 Poitiers, Fr. 47N 0
13 Poland (Ctry.) Eur. 52N 18E
11 Poltava, Ukr. 50N 35E
42 Pomona, Calif. 34N 118W
51 Ponce, P.R. 18N 67W
23 Pondicherry, India 12N 80E
28 Ponta Delgada, Port. 38N 26W
54 Ponta Grossa, Braz. 25S 50W
53 Ponta Pora, Braz. 22S 56W
36 Pontiac, Mich. 43N 83W
24 Pontianak, Indon. 0 109
52 Poopo, Lago de (L.) Bol. 18S 68W
52 Popayán, Col. 2N 77W
23 Porbandar, India 22N 70E
12 Pori, Fin. 61N 22E
17 Poronaysk, Russia 49N 143E
32 Port Alice, B.C., Can. 50N 127W
40 Port Angeles, Wash. 48N 123W
51 Port Antonio, Jam. 18N 76W
47 Port Arthur, Tex. 30N 94W
51 Port-au-Prince, Hai. 19N 72W
30 Port Elizabeth, S. Afr. 34S 26E
28 Port Harcourt, Nig. 5N 7E
36 Port Huron, Mich. 43N 82W
37 Portland, Maine 44N 70W
40 Portland, Oreg. 46N 123W
25 Port Moresby, Pap. N. Gui. 10S 147E
14 Porto, Port. 41N 9W
54 Porto Alegre, Braz. 30S 51W
51 Port of Spain, Trin. 11N 61W
28 Porto-Novo, Benin 7N 3E
52 Porto Velho, Braz. 9S 64W
32 Port Radium, N.W. Ter., Can. 66N 118W
29 Port Said, Eg. 31N 32E
13 Portsmouth, Eng. 51N 1W
37 Portsmouth, N.H. 43N 71W
36 Portsmouth, Ohio 39N 83W
37 Portsmouth, Va. 37N 76W
14 Portugal (Ctry.) Eur. 40N 8W
54 Posadas, Arg. 28S 56W
13 Potenza, It. 41N 16E
11 Poti, Geor. 42N 42E
37 Potomac (R.) U.S. 38N 77W
52 Potosí, Bol. 20S 66W
13 Potsdam, Ger. 52N 13E
37 Pottstown, Pa. 40N 76W
37 Pottsville, Pa. 41N 76W
37 Poughkeepsie, N.Y. 42N 74W
21 Poyang Hu (L.) China 29N 117E
13 Poznan, Pol. 52N 17E
13 Prague (Praha), Czech. 50N 14E
28 Praia, C.V. 15N 23W
13 Přerov, Czech. 49N 17E
43 Prescott, Ariz. 34N 112W
13 Prešov, Slov. 49N 21E
30 Pretoria, S. Afr. 26S 28E
15 Prilep, Mac. 41N 22E
32 Prince Albert, Sask., Can. 53N 106W
33 Prince Edward Island (Prov.) Can. 47N 63W
32 Prince George, B.C., Can. 54N 123W
32 Prince Rupert, B.C., Can. 54N 130W
15 Priština, Yugo. 43N 21E
15 Prizren, Yugo. 42N 21E
24 Prome (Pye), Mya. 19N 95E
37 Providence, R.I. 42N 71W
43 Provo, Utah 40N 112W
13 Przemysl, Pol. 50N 23E
20 Przheval'sk, Kyrg. 42N 78E
10 Pskov, Russia 58N 28E
50 Puebla, Mex. 19N 98W
44 Pueblo, Col. 38N 105W
54 Puerto Aisén, Chile 46S 73W
52 Puerto Cabello, Ven. 10N 68W
54 Puerto Deseado, Arg. 48S 66W
52 Puerto la Cruz, Ven. 10N 65W
14 Puertollano, Sp. 39N 4W
54 Puerto Natales, Chile 52S 72W
51 Puerto Rico (Ctry.) N.A. 18N 67W
54 Puerto Santa Cruz, Arg. 50S 69W
53 Puerto Suárez, Bol. 19S 58W
40 Puget Sound, Wash. 48N 122W
14 Pula, Cro. 45N 14E
23 Punakha, Bhu. 28N 90E
23 Pune, India 18N 72E
54 Punta Arenas, Chile 53S 71W
52 Punto Fijo, Ven. 12N 70W
23 Puri, India 20N 86E
21 Pusan, Kor. 35N 129E
11 Pyatigorsk, Russia 44N 43E
24 Pyinmana, Mya. 20N 96E
21 P'yŏngyang, Kor. 39N 126E
14 Pyrenees (Mts.), Fr.-Sp. 43N 0

Q

20 Qamdo, China 31N 97E
23 Qandahār, Afg. 32N 66E
16 Qaraghandy, Kaz. 50N 73E
16 Qarqaraly, Kaz. 49N 75E
29 Qaşr al Burayqah, Libya 30N 19E
22 Qatar (Ctry.) Asia 25N 51E
22 Qeshm, Iran 27N 56E
29 Qinā, Eg. 26N 33E
21 Qingdao, China 36N 120E
21 Qinhuangdao, China 40N 120E
21 Qiqihar, China 47N 124E
20 Qitai, China 44N 89E
22 Qom, Iran 34N 51E
22 Qomsheh, Iran 32N 52E
16 Qostanay, Kaz. 53N 64E
21 Quanzhou, China 25N 119E
33 Québec, Que., Can. 47N 71W
33 Quebec (Prov.) Can. 52N 70W
32 Queen Charlotte Is., B.C., Can. 54N 133W
50 Querétaro, Mex. 21N 100W
23 Quetta, Pak. 30N 67E
50 Quezaltenango, Guat. 15N 91W
25 Quezon City, Phil. 15N 121E
52 Quibdó, Col. 6N 77W
54 Quilmes, Arg. 34S 58W
23 Quilon, India 9N 76E
13 Quimper, Fr. 48N 4W
37 Quincy, Mass. 42N 71W
52 Quito, Ec. 0 79W
21 Quxian, China 29N 119E
16 Qyzylorda, Kaz. 45N 66E

R

28 Rabat, Mor. 34N 7W
39 Racine, Wis. 43N 88W
13 Radom, Pol. 51N 21E
54 Rafaela, Arg. 31S 61W
22 Rafḩā, Sau. Ar. 30N 43E
14 Ragusa, It. 37N 15E
23 Raigarh, India 22N 84E
40 Rainier, Mt., Wash. 47N 122W
33 Rainy River, Ont., Can. 49N 94W
23 Raipur, India 21N 82E
23 Rājahmundry, India 17N 82E
23 Rājkot, India 22N 71E
23 Rājshāhi, Pak. 24N 89E
49 Raleigh, N.C. 36N 79W
23 Rāmpur, India 29N 79E
54 Rancagua, Chile 34S 71W
23 Rānchī, India 23N 85E
12 Randers, Den. 56N 10E
46 Ranger, Tex. 32N 99W
24 Rangoon (Yangon), Mya. 17N 96E
23 Rangpur, Bngl. 26N 89E
38 Rapid City, S. Dak. 44N 103W
15 Rashīd, Eg. 31N 30E
22 Rasht, Iran 37N 50E
44 Raton, N. Mex. 37N 104W
13 Ravenna, It. 44N 12E
23 Rāwalpindi, Pak. 34N 73E
22 Rawāndūz, Iraq 37N 44E
41 Rawlins, Wyo. 42N 107W
54 Rawson, Arg. 43S 65W
13 Reading, Eng. 51N 1W
37 Reading, Pa. 40N 76W
53 Recife (Pernambuco), Braz. 8S 35W
32 Red (R.) Can.-U.S. 48N 97W
24 Red (R.) China-Viet. 21N 104E
34 Red (R.) U.S. 32N 93W
32 Red Deer, Alta., Can. 52N 114W
40 Redding, Calif. 40N 122W
22 Red Sea, Afr.-Asia 24N 37E
13 Regensburg, Ger. 49N 12E
13 Reggio di Calabria, It. 38N 16E
13 Reggio nell'Emilia, It. 45N 11E
32 Regina, Sask., Can. 51N 104W
13 Reims, Fr. 49N 4E
32 Reindeer L., Can. 58N 102W
13 Rennes, Fr. 48N 1W
42 Reno, Nev. 40N 120W
54 Resistencia, Arg. 27S 59W
9 Reunion (Ctry.), Ind. O. 22S 56E
14 Reus, Sp. 41N 1E
23 Rewa, India 25N 81E
12 Reykjavik, Ice. 64N 22W
13 Rhein (R.) Eur. 51N 7E
35 Rhode Island (State) U.S. 42N 72W
14 Rhône (R.) Fr.-Switz. 44N 5E
53 Ribeirão Prêto, Braz. 21S 48W
40 Richland, Wash. 46N 119W
37 Richmond, Va. 38N 77W
13 Rieti, It. 42N 13E
10 Rīga, Lat. 57N 24E
22 Rīgān, Iran 29N 59E
14 Rijeka, Cro. 45N 13E
13 Rimini, It. 44N 13E
12 Ringkobing, Den. 56N 8E
52 Ríobamba, Ec. 2S 79W
52 Rio Branco, Braz. 10S 68W
54 Río Cuarto, Arg. 33S 64W
54 Rio de Janeiro, Braz. 23S 43W
54 Río Gallegos, Arg. 52S 68W
54 Rio Grande, Braz. 31S 52W
34 Rio Grande (R.) Mex.-U.S. 26N 98W
28 Rio Muni (Polit. Reg.), Eq. Gui. 2N 10E
42 Riverside, Calif. 34N 117W
22 Riyadh, Sau. Ar. 25N 47E
15 Rize, Tur. 41N 40E
13 Roanne, Fr. 46N 4E
49 Roanoke, Va. 37N 80W
54 Rocha, Ur. 34S 54W
13 Rochefort, Fr. 46N 1W
39 Rochester, Minn. 44N 92W
37 Rochester, N.Y. 43N 78W
36 Rockford, Ill. 42N 89W
27 Rockhampton, Austl. 23S 150E
49 Rock Hill, S.C. 35N 81W
39 Rock Island, Ill. 42N 96W
41 Rock Springs, Wyo. 42N 109W
37 Rockville Centre, N.Y. 41N 74W
34 Rocky Mts., N.A. 45N 110W
15 Rodhós, Grc. 36N 28E
15 Romania (Ctry.) Eur. 46N 23E
48 Rome, Ga. 34N 85W
13 Rome, It. 42N 13E
54 Rosario, Arg. 33S 61W
40 Roseburg, Oreg. 43N 123W
13 Rosenheim, Ger. 48N 12E
12 Rostock, Ger. 54N 12E
11 Rostov-na-Donu, Russia 47N 40E
44 Roswell, N. Mex. 33N 105W
13 Rotterdam, Neth. 52N 4E
13 Rouen, Fr. 49N 22E
36 Royal Oak, Mich. 42N 83W
16 Rubtsovsk, Russia 52N 81E
29 Rudolf, L., Eth.-Ken. 4N 36E
28 Rufisque, Sen. 15N 17W
15 Ruse, Bul. 44N 26E
32 Russell, Man., Can. 51N 101W
16 Russia (Ctry.) Asia-Eur. 60N 80E
30 Rwanda (Ctry.) Afr. 2S 30E
11 Ryazan', Russia 55N 40E
11 Rybinsk, Russia 58N 39E
13 Rzeszow, Pol. 50N 22E
11 Rzhev, Russia 56N 34E

S

13 Saarbrücken, Ger. 49N 7E
15 Šabac, Yugo. 45N 20E
24 Sabah (Polit. Reg.), Mala. 5N 116E
47 Sabine (R.) U.S. 30N 94W
42 Sacramento, Calif. 39N 121W
42 Sacramento (R.) Calif. 38N 122W
15 Safad, Isr. 33N 35E
28 Safi (Asfi), Mor. 32N 9W
23 Sāgar, India 24N 79E
36 Saginaw, Mich. 43N 84W
33 Saguenay (R.) Que., Can. 48N 71W
14 Sagunto, Sp. 40N 0
28 Sahara (Des.) Afr. 23N 10E
23 Sahāranpur, India 30N 78E
28 Saïda, Alg. 35N 0
49 St. Agustine, Fla. 30N 81W
13 St. Brieuc, Fr. 49N 3W
33 St. Catharines, Ont., Can. 43N 79W
37 St. Clair, L., Can.-U.S. 42N 83W
39 St. Cloud, Minn. 46N 94W
13 St. Denis, Fr. 40N 2E
13 St. Étienne, Fr. 45N 4E
33 St. George's, Newf., Can. 48N 58W
13 St. George's Chan., Eur. 52N 7W
8 St. Helena (Ctry.), Atl. O. 15S 10W
40 St. Helens, Mt. (Vol.) Wash. 46N 122W
33 St. Hyacinthe, Que., Can. 46N 73W
33 St. John, N.B., Can. 45N 66W
33 St. John's, Newf., Can. 48N 53W
45 St. Joseph, Mo. 40N 95W
51 St. Kitts and Nevis (Ctry.) N.A. 17N 63W
33 St. Lawrence (R.) Can.-U.S. 48N 69W
33 St. Lawrence, G. of, Can. 48N 62W
45 St. Louis, Mo. 39N 90W
28 St. Louis, Sen. 16N 16W
51 St. Lucia (Ctry.) N.A. 14N 61W
13 St. Malo, Fr. 49N 2W
13 St. Nazaire, Fr. 48N 2W
32 St. Paul, Alta., Can. 54N 111W
39 St. Paul, Minn. 45N 93W
49 St. Petersburg, Fla. 28N 83W
10 St. Petersburg (Leningrad), Russia 60N 30E
33 St. Pierre and Miquelon (Ctry.) N.A. 47N 57W
13 St. Quentin, Fr. 50N 3E
51 St. Vincent and the Grenadines (Ctry.) N.A. 13N 61W
22 Sakākah, Sau. Ar. 30N 40E
14 Salamanca, Sp. 41N 6W
28 Salé, Mor. 34N 7W
16 Salekhard, Russia 67N 67E
23 Salem, India 12N 78E
37 Salem, Mass. 43N 71W
40 Salem, Oreg. 45N 123W
13 Salerno, It. 40N 15E
45 Salina, Kans. 39N 98W
50 Salina Cruz, Mex. 16N 95W
42 Salinas, Calif. 37N 122W
13 Salisbury, Eng. 51N 2W
54 Salta, Arg. 25S 65W
43 Salt Lake City, Utah 41N 112W
54 Salto, Ur. 31S 58W
42 Salton Sea (L.) Calif. 33N 116W
53 Salvador (Bahia), Braz. 13S 38W
24 Salween (R.) Asia 21N 98E
13 Salzburg, Aus. 48N 13E
11 Samara, Russia 53N 50E
16 Samarkand, Uzb. 40N 67E
15 Samsun, Tur. 41N 36E
22 San'ā', Yemen 16N 44E
22 Sanandaj, Iran 36N 47E
46 San Angelo, Tex. 31N 100W
46 San Antonio, Tex. 29N 98W
54 San Antonio Oeste, Arg. 41S 65W
42 San Bernardino, Calif. 34N 117W
54 San Bernardo, Chile 34S 71W
51 Sánchez, Dom. Rep. 19N 70W
52 San Cristóbal, Ven. 8N 72W
51 Sancti Spíritus, Cuba 22N 79W
42 San Diego, Calif. 33N 117W
40 Sandpoint, Idaho 48N 116W
36 Sandusky, Ohio 41N 83W
54 San Fernando, Arg. 34S 59W
25 San Fernando, Phil. 17N 120E
49 Sanford, Fla. 29N 81W
54 San Francisco, Arg. 31S 62W
42 San Francisco, Calif. 38N 122W
23 Sāngli, India 17N 75E
54 San Isidro, Arg. 34S 59W
41 San Joaquin (R.) Calif. 37N 121W
42 San Jose, Calif. 37N 122W
51 San José, C.R. 10N 84W
51 San Juan, P.R. 18N 66W
54 San Justo, Arg. 34S 59W
13 Sankt Gallen, Switz. 47N 9E
15 Şanlıurfa, Tur. 37N 39E
14 Sanlúcar de Barramedo, Sp. 37N 6W
54 San Luis, Arg. 33S 66W
42 San Luis Obispo, Calif. 35N 121W
50 San Luis Potosí, Mex. 22N 101W
13 San Marino (Ctry.) Eur. 44N 13E
50 San Miguel, Sal. 13N 88W
54 San Nicolas, Arg. 33S 60W
54 San Rafael, Arg. 34S 68W
50 San Salvador, Sal. 14N 89W
14 San Sebastián, Sp. 43N 2W
42 Santa Ana, Calif. 34N 118W
50 Santa Ana, Sal. 14N 90W
42 Santa Barbara, Calif. 34N 120W
51 Santa Clara, Cuba 22N 80W
52 Santa Cruz, Bol. 18S 63W
54 Santa Cruz, Braz. 30S 52W
42 Santa Cruz, Calif. 37N 122W
28 Santa Cruz de Tenerife, Sp. 28N 15W
54 Santa Fe, Arg. 32S 61W
43 Santa Fe, N. Mex. 35N 106W
52 Santa Fe de Bogotá, Col. 5N 74W
54 Santa Lucia, Ur. 34S 56W
54 Santa Maria, Braz. 30S 54W
52 Santa Marta, Col. 11N 74W
42 Santa Monica, Calif. 34N 118W
54 Santa Rosa, Arg. 37S 64W
14 Santander, Sp. 43N 4W
42 Santa Rosa, Calif. 38N 123W
54 Santiago, Chile 33S 71W
14 Santiago de Campostela, Sp. 43N 9W
51 Santiago de Cuba, Cuba 20N 76W
54 Santiago del Estero, Arg. 28S 64W
51 Santo Domingo, Dom. Rep. 18N 70W
54 Santos, Braz. 24S 46W
53 São Carlos, Braz. 22S 48W
53 São Francisco (R.) Braz. 9S 40W
54 São Gonçalo, Braz. 23S 43W
54 São João del Rei, Braz. 21S 44W
54 São João de Meriti, Braz. 23S 43W
53 São Luis (Maranhão), Braz. 3S 43W
13 Saone (R.) Fr. 46N 5E
54 São Paulo, Braz. 24S 47W
54 São Vicente, Braz. 24S 46W
28 Sapele, Nig. 6N 5E

Traverse City, Mich. 63

21 Sapporo, Japan 43N 141 E
15 Sarajevo, Bos. 43N 18 E
54 Sarandi, Arg. 34S 58W
31 Saranley, Som. 2N 42 E
11 Saransk, Russia 54N 45 E
11 Sarapul, Russia 56N 54 E
49 Sarasota, Fla. 27N 83W
11 Saratov, Russia 52N 45 E
24 Sarawak (Polit. Reg.), Mala. 3N 113 E
13 Sardinia (I.) It. 40N 9 E
33 Sarnia, Ont., Can. 43N 82W
23 Sasarām, India 25N 84 E
21 Sasebo, Japan 33N 130 E
32 Saskatchewan (Prov.) Can. 55N 108W
32 Saskatchewan (R.) Can. 54N 103W
32 Saskatoon, Sask., Can. 52N 107W
13 Sassari, It. 41N 9 E
15 Satu-Mare, Rom. 48N 23 E
12 Saudarkrokur, Ice. 66N 20W
22 Saudi Arabia (Ctry.) Asia 27N 42 E
49 Savannah, Ga. 32N 81W
49 Savannah (R.) U.S. 33N 82W
13 Savona, It. 44N 8 E
29 Sawhāj, Eg. 27N 32 E
22 Sayḩūt, Yemen 15N 51 E
20 Sayr Usa, Mong. 45N 107 E
22 Say'un, Yemen 16N 49 E
13 Schaffhausen, Switz. 48N 9 E
37 Schenectady, N.Y. 43N 74W
12 Schleswig, Ger. 55N 10 E
12 Scotland (Polit. Reg.), U.K. 57N 3W
38 Scottsbluff, Nebr. 42N 104W
37 Scranton, Pa. 42N 76W
40 Seattle, Wash. 48N 122W
45 Sedalia, Mo. 39N 93W
14 Segovia, Sp. 41N 4W
13 Seine (R.) Fr. 49N 1 E
28 Sekondi-Takoradi, Ghana 5N 2W
32 Selkirk Mts., B.C., Can. 51N 117W
48 Selma, Ala. 32N 87W
52 Selvas (Reg.) Braz. 5S 64W
24 Semarang, Indon. 7S 110 E
16 Semey, Kaz. 50N 80 E
16 Semipalatinsk, see Semey, Kaz. 50N 80 E
21 Sendai, Japan 38N 141 E
28 Senegal (Ctry.) Afr. 15N 15W
21 Seoul (Sŏul), Kor. 38N 127 E
33 Sept-Îles, Que., Can. 50N 66W
15 Serbia (Rep.) Yugo. 44N 21 E
11 Serov, Russia 60N 60 E
11 Serpukhov, Russia 55N 37 E
15 Sérrai, Grc. 41N 24 E
28 Settat, Mor. 33N 7W
14 Setúbal, Port. 39N 9W
11 Sevastopol', Ukr. 45N 34 E
17 Severnaya Zemlya (Is.) Russia 79N 100 E
14 Sevilla, Sp. 37N 6W
9 Seychelles (Ctry.), Ind. O. 4S 55 E
31 Seylac, Som. 11N 43 E
31 Sezela, S. Afr. 30S 30 E
28 Sfax, Tun. 35N 11 E
31 Shabelle (R.) Som. 0N 43 E
20 Shache (Yarkand), China 38N 77 E
23 Shāhjahānpur, India 28N 80 E
16 Shakhrisyabz, Uzb. 39N 68 E
11 Shakhty, Russia 48N 40 E
16 Shalqar, Kaz. 48N 60 E
21 Shanghai, China 31N 121 E
20 Shanshan, China 43N 90 E
21 Shantou, China 23N 117 E
21 Shaoguan, China 25N 114 E
21 Shaoxing, China 30N 121 E
21 Shaoyang, China 27N 112 E
36 Sharon, Pa. 41N 80W
32 Shaunavon, Sask., Can. 50N 108W
45 Shawnee, Okla. 35N 97W
39 Sheboygan, Wis. 44N 88W
13 Sheffield, Eng. 53N 1W
16 Shenkursk, Russia 62N 43 E
21 Shenyang, China 42N 123 E
33 Sherbrooke, Que., Can. 45N 72W
41 Sheridan, Wyo. 45N 107W
45 Sherman, Tex. 34N 97W
12 Shetland Is., Scot. 60N 2W
22 Shibām, Yemen 16N 49 E
15 Shibīn al Kawm, Eg. 31N 31 E
21 Shijiazhuang, China 38N 115 E
23 Shikārpur, Pak. 28N 69 E
21 Shikoku (I.) Japan 33N 135 E
23 Shillong, India 26N 92 E
31 Shimber Berris (Mt.) Som. 11N 47 E
21 Shimonoseki, Japan 34N 131 E
22 Shīrāz, Iran 30N 52 E
23 Shivpuri, India 26N 78 E
15 Shkoder, Alb. 42N 19 E
23 Sholāpur, India 18N 76 E
47 Shreveport, La. 32N 94W
21 Shuangliao, China 44N 123 E
15 Shumen, Bul. 43N 27 E
22 Shuqrah, Yemen 14N 46 E
22 Shūshtar, Iran 32N 49 E
16 Shuya, Russia 57N 41 E
16 Shyghys Qongyrat, Kaz. 47N 75 E
16 Shymkent, Kaz. 42N 70 E
23 Siālkot, Pak. 33N 74 E
12 Šiauliai, Lith. 56N 23 E
15 Šibenik, Cro. 44N 16 E
15 Sibiu, Rom. 46N 24 E
24 Sibolga, Indon. 2N 99 E
13 Sicily (I.) It. 37N 14 E
28 Sidi bel Abbès, Alg. 35N 1W
28 Sidi Ifni, Mor. 29N 10W
13 Siena, It. 43N 11 E
28 Sierra Leone (Ctry.) Afr. 9N 13W
42 Sierra Nevada (Mts.) Calif. 38N 120W
15 Silifke, Tur. 36N 34 E
15 Silistra, Bul. 44N 27 E
37 Silver Spring, Md. 39N 77W
11 Simferopol', Ukr. 45N 34 E
23 Simla, India 31N 77 E
24 Singapore (Ctry.) Asia 1N 104 E
15 Sinop, Tur. 42N 35 E
21 Sinŭiju, Kor. 40N 125 E
38 Sioux City, Iowa 42N 96W
38 Sioux Falls, S. Dak. 44N 97W
33 Sioux Lookout, Ont., Can. 50N 92W
32 Sipiwesk, Man., Can. 56N 97W
15 Siracusa, It. 37N 15 E
23 Sirājganj, Bngl. 25N 90 E
15 Sisak, Cro. 45N 16 E
20 Sittwe, Mya. 20N 93 E
15 Sivas, Tur. 40N 37 E
12 Skagerrak (Str.) Den.-Nor. 57N 8 E
12 Skelleftea, Swe. 65N 21 E
28 Skikda, Alg. 37N 7 E
15 Skopje, Mac. 42N 21 E
17 Skovorodino, Russia 54N 124 E
16 Slavgorod, Russia 53N 79 E
15 Slavonski Brod, Cro. 45N 18 E
12 Sligo, Ire. 54N 8W
15 Sliven, Bul. 43N 26 E
16 Slobodskoy, Russia 59N 50 E
13 Slovakia (Ctry.) Eur. 48N 20 E
14 Slovenia (Ctry.) Eur. 46N 15 E
12 Slupsk, Pol. 54N 17 E
15 Smila, Ukr. 49N 32 E
32 Smith, Alta., Can. 55N 114W
11 Smolensk, Russia 55N 32 E
40 Snake (R.) U.S. 45N 117W
11 Sochi, Russia 44N 40 E
15 Sofia (Sofiya), Bul. 43N 23 E
15 Söke, Tur. 38N 27 E
28 Sokoto, Nig. 13N 5 E
11 Solikamsk, Russia 60N 57 E
16 Sol'-Iletsk, Russia 51N 55 E
27 Solomon Islands (Ctry.) Pac. O. 7S 160 E
31 Somalia (Ctry.) Afr. 3N 43 E
15 Sombor, Yugo. 46N 19 E
37 Somerville, Mass. 42N 71W
21 Songjiang, China 31N 121 E
24 Songkhla, Thai. 7N 101 E
13 Sopron, Hung. 48N 17 E
16 Sortavala, Russia 62N 31 E
16 Sosnogorsk, Russia 63N 54 E
14 Souq-Ahras, Alg. 36N 8 E
32 Souris, Man., Can. 50N 100W
28 Sousse, Tun. 36N 11 E
30 South Africa (Ctry.) Afr. 28S 28 E
36 South Bend, Ind. 42N 86W
35 South Carolina (State) U.S. 34N 81W
21 South China Sea, Asia 20N 114 E
34 South Dakota (State) U.S. 44N 102W
27 Southern Alps (Mts.) N.Z. 44S 169 E
13 Southhampton, Eng. 51N 1W
33 Southhampton (I.) N.W. Ter., Can. 65N 85W
27 South I., N.Z. 43S 167 E
32 South Saskatchewan (R.) Can. 50N 110W
12 South Shields, Eng. 55N 1W
12 Sovetsk (Tilsit), Russia 55N 22 E
17 Sovetskaya Gavan', Russia 49N 140 E
14 Spain (Ctry.) Eur. 40N 4W
49 Spartanburg, S.C. 35N 82W
17 Spassk-Dal'niy, Russia 44N 133 E
15 Split, Cro. 43N 16 E
40 Spokane, Wash. 48N 117W
15 Spola, Ukr. 49N 32 E
36 Springfield, Ill. 40N 90W
37 Springfield, Mass. 42N 73W
45 Springfield, Mo. 37N 93W
36 Springfield, Ohio 40N 84W
17 Sredne-Kolymsk, Russia 68N 155 E
23 Sri Lanka (Ceylon) (Ctry.) Asia 7N 79 E
23 Srīnagar, India 34N 75 E
37 Stamford, Conn. 41N 74W
54 Stanley, Falk. Is. 52S 58W
15 Stara Zagora, Bul. 42N 26 E
12 Stargard Szczeciński, Pol. 53N 15 E
12 Stavanger, Nor. 59N 6 E
16 Stepn'ak, Kaz. 53N 71 E
44 Sterling, Col. 41N 103W
11 Sterlitamak, Russia 54N 56 E
32 Stettler, Alta., Can. 52N 113W
36 Steubenville, Ohio 40N 81W
27 Stewart (I.) N.Z. 47S 168 E
28 Stif, Alg. 36N 5 E
32 Stikine Ranges, Can. 59N 129W
12 Stockholm, Swe. 59N 18 E
42 Stockton, Calif. 38N 121W
13 Stoke-on-Trent, Eng. 53N 2W
12 Stralsund, Ger. 54N 13 E
13 Strasbourg, Fr. 49N 8 E
37 Stratford, Conn. 41N 73W
36 Stratford, Ont., Can. 43N 81W
15 Strumica, Mac. 41N 23 E
15 Stryy, Ukr. 49N 24 E
13 Stuttgart, Ger. 49N 9 E
25 Subic, Phil. 15N 120 E
15 Subotica, Yugo. 46N 20 E
52 Sucre, Bol. 19S 65W
29 Sudan (Ctry.) Afr. 15N 29 E
33 Sudbury, Ont., Can. 46N 81W
13 Sudetes (Mts.) Czech Rep.-Pol. 51N 16 E
29 Suez (As Suways), Eg. 30N 33 E
29 Suez, G. of, Eg. 29N 33 E
29 Suez Canal, Eg. 30N 32 E
21 Suifenhe, China 45N 131 E
24 Sukabumi, Indon. 7S 107 E
11 Sukhumi, Geor. 43N 41 E
23 Sukkur, Pak. 28N 69 E
15 Sulina, Rom. 45N 30 E
24 Sulu Sea, Mala.-Phil. 9N 119 E
24 Sumatra (Sumatera) (I.) Indon. 2N 100 E
24 Sumba (I.) Indon. 10S 119 E
12 Sunderland, Eng. 55N 1W
12 Sundsvall, Swe. 62N 19 E
11 Sumy, Ukr. 51N 35 E
17 Suntar, Russia 62N 118 E
39 Superior, Wis. 47N 92W
39 Superior, L., Can.-U.S. 48N 88W
15 Şūr (Tyre), Leb. 33N 35 E
22 Şūr, Oman 22N 59 E
24 Surabaya, Indon. 7S 113 E
24 Surakarta, Indon. 8S 111 E
23 Surat, India 21N 73 E
16 Surgut, Russia 61N 74 E
53 Suriname (Ctry.) S.A. 4N 56W
29 Surt, Libya 31N 17 E
37 Susquehanna (R.) U.S. 40N 76W
21 Suzhou, China 31N 121 E
16 Svalbard (Is.) Nor. 74N 20 E
11 Sverdlovsk, see Yekaterinburg, Russia 57N 61 E
17 Svobodnyy, Russia 51N 128 E
13 Swansea, Wales 52N 4W
30 Swaziland (Ctry.) Afr. 27S 31 E
12 Sweden (Ctry.) Eur. 60N 14 E
46 Sweetwater, Tex. 32N 100W
13 Switzerland (Ctry.) Eur. 47N 8 E
27 Sydney, Austl. 34S 151 E
16 Syktyvkar, Russia 61N 50 E
15 Synel'nykove, Ukr. 48N 36 E
37 Syracuse, N.Y. 43N 76W
16 Syr Darya (R.) Asia 46N 61 E
22 Syria (Ctry.) Asia 34N 38 E
11 Syzran', Russia 53N 48 E
12 Szczecin (Stettin), Pol. 53N 15 E
12 Szczecinek, Pol. 54N 17 E
13 Szeged, Hung. 46N 20 E
13 Székesfehérvár, Hung. 47N 18 E
13 Szolnok, Hung. 47N 20 E
13 Szombathely, Hung. 47N 17 E

T

22 Tabrīz, Iran 38N 46 E
20 Tacheng, China 47N 83 E
25 Tacloban, Phil. 11N 125 E
40 Tacoma, Wash. 47N 122W
54 Tacuarembó, Ur. 32S 56W
22 Tadjoura, Djibouti 12N 43 E
21 Taegu, Kor. 36N 129 E
11 Taganrog, Russia 47N 39 E
14 Tagus (R.) Port.-Sp. 39N 8W
42 Tahoe, L., U.S. 39N 120W
21 T'aichung, Taiwan 24N 121 E
21 T'ainan, Taiwan 23N 120 E
21 T'aipei, Taiwan 25N 121 E
21 Taiwan (Formosa) (Ctry.) Asia 23N 122 E
21 Taiwan Strait, China-Taiwan 25N 120 E
21 Taiyuan, China 38N 113 E
23 Tajikistan (Ctry.) Asia 39N 71 E
24 Tak, Thai. 16N 99 E
21 Takamatsu, Japan 34N 134 E
20 Takla Makan (Des.) China 39N 82 E
25 Talasea, Pap. N. Gui. 5S 150 E
54 Talca, Chile 35S 72W
54 Talcahuano, Chile 37S 73W
48 Tallahassee, Fla. 30N 84W
10 Tallinn, Est. 59N 25 E
11 Tambov, Russia 53N 41 E
49 Tampa, Fla. 28N 82W
12 Tampere, Fin. 62N 24W
50 Tampico, Mex. 22N 98W
54 Tandil, Arg. 37S 59W
30 Tanganyika, L., Afr. 6S 30 E
28 Tanger, Mor. 36N 6W
24 Tanjungkarang-Telukbetung, Indon. 5S 105 E
22 Tannūrah, Ra's at (C.) Sau. Ar. 27N 50 E
29 Ţantā, Eg. 31N 31 E
30 Tanzania (Ctry.) Afr. 7S 33 E
21 Tao'an, China 45N 123 E
53 Tapajós (R.) Braz. 3S 56W
16 Tara, Russia 57N 74 E
22 Ţarābulus (Tripoli), Leb. 34N 36 E
13 Taranto, It. 40N 17 E
13 Tarbes, Fr. 43N 0
14 Tarifa, Sp. 36N 6W
22 Tarīm, Yemen 16N 49 E
28 Tarkwa, Ghana 5N 2W
13 Tarnow, Pol. 50N 21 E
14 Tarragona, Sp. 41N 1 E
15 Tarsus, Tur. 37N 35 E
10 Tartu, Est. 58N 27 E
15 Ţarţūs, Syr. 35N 36 E
16 Tashkent, Uzb. 41N 69 E
27 Tasmania (I.) Austl. 42S 147 E
27 Tasman Sea, Oc. 37S 155 E
16 Tatarsk, Russia 55N 75 E
21 Tatar Str., Russia 50N 141 E
53 Taubate, Braz. 23S 46W
37 Taunton, Mass. 42N 71W
16 Tavda, Russia 58N 65 E
22 Taymā', Sau. Ar. 28N 39 E
16 Tazovskoye, Russia 67N 78 E
28 Tbessa, Alg. 35N 8 E
11 Tbilisi, Geor. 42N 45 E
12 Tczew, Pol. 54N 19 E
15 Tecuci, Rom. 46N 27 E
50 Tegucigalpa, Hond. 14N 87W
22 Tehrān, Iran 36N 51 E
50 Tehuantepec, Golfo de (G.) Mex. 16N 95W
15 Tekirdağ, Tur. 41N 27 E
22 Tel Aviv-Yafo, Isr. 32N 35 E
16 Temīr, Kaz. 49N 57 E
16 Temīrtau, Kaz. 50N 73 E
43 Tempe, Ariz. 33N 112W
47 Temple, Tex. 31N 97W
15 Temryuk, Russia 45N 37 E
54 Temuco, Chile 39S 73W
35 Tennessee (State) U.S. 36N 88W
50 Tepic, Mex. 22N 105W
53 Teresina, Braz. 5S 43W
54 Teresópolis, Braz. 22S 43W
23 Termez, Uzb. 37N 67 E
13 Terni, It. 43N 13 E
15 Ternopil', Ukr. 50N 26 E
32 Terrace, B.C., Can. 55N 129W
13 Terracina, It. 41N 13 E
36 Terre Haute, Ind. 39N 87W
28 Tetouan, Mor. 36N 6W
15 Tetovo, Mac. 42N 21 E
45 Texarkana, Ark. 33N 94W
34 Texas (State) U.S. 31N 101W
47 Texas City, Tex. 29N 95W
24 Thailand (Ctry.) Asia 16N 101 E
24 Thailand, G. of, Asia 12N 101 E
13 Thames (R.) Eng. 51N 1 E
24 Thanh Hoa, Viet. 20N 106 E
23 Thanjāvūr, India 11N 79 E
40 The Dalles, Oreg. 46N 121W
49 The Everglades (Swamp) Fla. 26N 81W
13 The Hague ('s Gravenhage), Neth. 52N 4 E
15 Thessaloníki, Grc. 41N 23 E
28 Thiès, Sen. 15N 17W
20 Thimphu, Bhu. 28N 90 E
13 Thionville, Fr. 49N 6 E
15 Thivai (Thebes), Grc. 38N 23 E
30 Thohoyandou, Venda 23S 31 E
32 Thompson, Man., Can. 56N 98W
33 Thunder Bay, Ont., Can. 48N 89W
21 Tianjin, China 39N 117 E
15 Tiberias, Isr. 33N 36 E
20 Tibet, Plateau of, China 32N 83 E
21 Tieling, China 42N 124 E
20 Tien Shan (Mts.) Asia 43N 80 E
54 Tierra del Fuego (I.) Arg.-Chile 54S 68W
54 Tigre, Arg. 34S 58W
28 Tihert, Alg. 35N 1 E
50 Tijuana, Mex. 33N 117W
15 Tikhoretsk, Russia 46N 40 E
16 Tikhvin, Russia 60N 34 E
22 Tikrīt, Iraq 35N 44 E
17 Tiksi, Russia 72N 129 E
13 Tilburg, Neth. 52N 5 E
28 Tilimsen, Alg. 35N 1W
15 Timashevskaya, Russia 46N 38 E
15 Timişoara, Rom. 46N 21 E
33 Timmins, Ont., Can. 48N 81W
25 Timor (I.) Indon. 10S 125 E
25 Timor Sea, Austl.-Indon. 10S 128 E
28 Tindouf, Alg. 28N 8W
15 Tiranë, Alb. 41N 20 E
15 Tiraspol, Mol. 47N 30 E
15 Tîrgoviste, Rom. 45N 25 E
15 Tîrgu-Jiu, Rom. 45N 23 E
15 Tîrgu-Mureş, Rom. 47N 25 E
23 Tiruchchirāppalli, India 11N 79 E
23 Tirunelveli, India 8N 78 E
32 Tisdale, Sask., Can. 53N 104W
13 Tisza (R.) Eur. 46N 20 E
52 Titicaca, Lago (L.) Bol.-Peru 16S 69W
13 Tivoli, It. 42N 13 E
50 Tlaxcala, Mex. 19N 98W
31 Toamasina, Mad. 18S 49 E
18 Tobol'sk, Russia 59N 68 E
53 Tocantins (R.) Braz. 3S 50W
54 Tocopilla, Chile 22S 70W
28 Togo (Ctry.) Afr. 8N 1 E
15 Tokat, Tur. 40N 36 E
8 Tokelau (Ctry.), Pac. O. 8S 172W
16 Tokmak, Kyrg. 43N 76 E
21 Tokushima, Japan 34N 135 E
21 Tōkyō, Japan 36N 140 E
36 Toledo, Ohio 42N 84W
14 Toledo, Sp. 40N 4W
50 Toluca, Mex. 19N 100W
17 Tommot, Russia 59N 126 E
16 Tomsk, Russia 56N 85 E
8 Tonga (Ctry.), Pac. O. 20S 173W
21 Tonghua, China 42N 126 E
20 Tongren, China 27N 110 E
23 Tonk, India 26N 76 E
24 Tonkin, G. of, China-Viet. 20N 107 E
42 Tonopah, Nev. 38N 117W
45 Topeka, Kans. 39N 96W
16 Torghay, Kaz. 50N 64 E
33 Toronto, Ont., Can. 44N 79W
50 Torréon, Mex. 26N 103W
37 Torrington, Conn. 42N 73W
12 Torun, Pol. 53N 19 E
28 Touggourt, Alg. 33N 6 E
13 Toul, Fr. 49N 6 E
13 Toulon, Fr. 43N 6 E
13 Toulouse, Fr. 44N 1 E
24 Toungoo, Mya. 19N 96 E
13 Tours, Fr. 47N 1 E
21 Toyama, Japan 37N 137 E
15 Trabzon, Tur. 41N 40 E
30 Transkei (Ctry.) Afr. 31S 29 E
13 Trapani, It. 38N 12 E
36 Traverse City, Mich. 45N 86W

13	Trento, It.	46N	11 E
37	Trenton, N.J.	40N	75W
54	Tres Arroyos, Arg.	38S	60W
13	Treviso, It.	46N	12 E
13	Trier, Ger.	50N	7 E
13	Trieste, It.	46N	14 E
15	Trikkala, Grc.	40N	22 E
23	Trincomalee, Sri Lanka . .	9N	81 E
44	Trinidad, Col.	37N	105W
51	Trinidad and Tobago		
	(Ctry.) N.A.	11N	61W
47	Trinity (R.) Tex.	31N	95W
52	Tripoli, Libya	33N	13 E
23	Trivandrum, India	8N	77 E
33	Trois-Rivières, Que., Can.	46N	73W
11	Troitsk, Russia	54N	62 E
16	Troitsko-Pechorsk, Russia	62N	56 E
12	Trondheim (Nidaros), Nor.		
	. . . .	63N	12 E
37	Troy, N.Y.	43N	74W
13	Troyes, Fr.	48N	4 E
15	Trstenik, Yugo.	44N	20 E
52	Trujillo, Peru	8S	79W
52	Trujillo, Ven.	9N	70W
31	Tsiafajovona (Mt.) Mad.	19S	47 E
15	Tuapse, Russia	44N	39 E
52	Tubruq (Tobruk), Libya	32N	24 E
52	Tucacas, Ven.	11N	68W
43	Tucson, Ariz.	32N	111W
54	Tucumán, Arg.	27S	65W
11	Tula, Russia	54N	38 E
15	Tulcea, Rom.	45N	29 E
45	Tulsa, Okla.	36N	96W
11	Tulun, Russia	54N	101 E
28	Tunis, Tun.	37N	10 E
28	Tunisia (Ctry.) Afr.	35N	10 E
52	Tunja, Col.	5N	73W
17	Tura, Russia	64N	100 E
13	Turin, It.	45N	8 E
16	Turkestan (Reg.) Asia . .	43N	65 E
11	Turkey (Ctry.) Asia-Eur. .	38N	33 E
22	Turkmenistan (Ctry.) Asia	40N	60 E
12	Turku, Fin.	60N	22 E
15	Turnu-Severin, Rom. . . .	45N	23 E
20	Turpan, China	43N	89 E
17	Turukhansk, Russia	66N	89 E
48	Tuscaloosa, Ala.	33N	88W
9	Tuvalu (Ctry.), Pac. O. . .	8S	177 E
50	Tuxtla Gutiérrez, Mex. . .	17N	93W
15	Tuzla, Bos.	45N	19 E
11	Tver', Russia	57N	36 E
41	Twin Falls, Idaho	43N	114W
47	Tyler, Tex.	32N	95W
17	Tyndinskiy, Russia	55N	125 E
13	Tynemouth, Eng.	55N	2W
13	Tyrrhenian Sea, Fr.-It. . .	40N	11 E
16	Tyukalinsk, Russia	56N	72 E
16	Tyumen', Russia	57N	65 E

U

29	Ubangi (R.) Afr.	3N	18 E
53	Uberaba, Braz.	20S	48W
53	Uberlândia, Braz.	19S	48W
23	Udaipur, India	25N	74 E
13	Udine, It.	46N	13 E
11	Ufa, Russia	55N	56 E
29	Uganda (Ctry.) Afr.	2N	32 E
21	Uiju, Kor.	40N	125 E
23	Ujjain, India	23N	76 E
24	Ujungpandang (Makasar),		
	Indon.	5S	119 E
11	Ukraine (Ctry.) Eur.	49N	32 E
20	Ulaangom, Mong.	50N	92 E
21	Ulan Bator, Mong.	47N	107 E
17	Ulan-Ude, Russia	52N	108 E
15	Ulcinj, Yugo.	42N	19 E
20	Uliastay, Mong.	48N	97 E
13	Ulm, Ger.	48N	10 E
11	Ul'yanovsk, Russia	54N	48 E
30	Umtata, Transkei	32S	28 E
22	Unayzah, Sau. Ar.	26N	44 E
22	United Arab Emirates		
	(Ctry.) Asia	23N	53 E
12	United Kingdom (Ctry.)		
	Eur.	55N	3W
34	United States (Ctry.) N.A.	38N	100W
12	Uppsala, Swe.	60N	18 E
11	Ural (R.) Kaz.-Russia . . .	50N	52 E
16	Urals (Mts.) Russia	62N	60 E
32	Uranium City, Sask., Can.	60N	109W
36	Urbana, Ill.	40N	88W
54	Uruguaiana, Braz.	30S	57W
54	Uruguay (Ctry.) S.A. . . .	33S	56W
54	Uruguay (R.) S.A.	28S	55W
20	Ürümqi, China	44N	88 E
15	Usak, Tur.	39N	29 E
54	Ushuaia, Arg.	55S	68W
17	Ussuriysk, Russia	44N	132 E
17	Ust'-Kulom, Russia	62N	54 E
17	Ust'-Maya, Russia	61N	135 E
17	Ust'-Oleněk, Russia	73N	120 E
16	Ust' Port, Russia	69N	84 E
16	Ust'-Tsil'ma, Russia	65N	52 E
17	Ust' Tyrma, Russia	50N	131 E
20	Usu, China	44N	84 E
34	Utah (State) U.S.	39N	113W
37	Utica, N.Y.	43N	75W
13	Utrecht, Neth.	52N	5 E
14	Utrera, Sp.	37N	6W
21	Utsunomiya, Japan	37N	140 E
24	Uttaradit, Thai.	18N	100 E
22	Uzbekistan (Ctry.) Asia . .	41N	64 E

V

12	Vaasa, Fin.	63N	22 E
13	Vác, Hung.	48N	19 E
12	Vadsö, Nor.	70N	30 E
14	Valdepeñas, Sp.	39N	3W
54	Valdivia, Chile	40S	73W
48	Valdosta, Ga.	31N	83W
13	Valence, Fr.	45N	5 E
14	Valencia, Sp.	39N	0
52	Valencia, Ven.	10N	68W
38	Valentine, Nebr.	43N	101W
14	Valladolid, Sp.	42N	5W
42	Vallejo, Calif.	38N	122W
13	Valletta, Malta	36N	15 E
38	Valley City, N. Dak.	47N	98W
54	Valparaíso, Chile	33S	72W
32	Vancouver, B.C., Can. . .	49N	123W
40	Vancouver, Wash.	46N	123W
32	Vancouver I., B.C., Can.	50N	127W
13	Vannes, Fr.	48N	3W
27	Vanuatu (Ctry.) Pac. O. .	17S	169 E
23	Vārānāsi (Benaras), India	25N	83 E
13	Varaždin, Cro.	46N	16 E
15	Varna (Stalin), Bul.	43N	28 E
12	Vasterås, Swe.	60N	17 E
13	Vatican City (Ctry.) Eur. .	42N	12 E
32	Vegreville, Alta., Can. . .	53N	112W
16	Velikiy Ustyug, Russia . .	61N	47 E
16	Veliko Turnovo, Bul. . . .	43N	26 E
23	Vellore, India	13N	79 E
16	Vel'sk, Russia	61N	42 E
30	Venda (Ctry.) Afr.	23S	31 E
52	Venezuela (Ctry.) S.A. . .	8N	65W
13	Venice, It.	45N	12 E
12	Ventspils, Lat.	57N	21 E
50	Veracruz, Mex.	19N	96W
23	Verāval, India	21N	70 E
13	Verdun, Fr.	49N	5 E
32	Vermilion, Alta., Can. . .	53N	111W
35	Vermont (State) U.S. . . .	44N	73W
13	Verona, It.	45N	11 E
13	Versailles, Fr.	49N	2 E
13	Vesuvio (Vol.) It.	41N	15 E
24	Viangchan, Laos	18N	103 E
54	Vicente López, Arg.	34S	58W
13	Vicenza, It.	46N	12 E
13	Vichy, Fr.	46N	3 E
48	Vicksburg, Miss.	32N	91W
32	Victoria, B.C., Can. . . .	48N	123W
31	Victoria, L., Afr.	1S	33 E
30	Victoria Falls, Zambia-		
	Zimb.	18S	25 E
32	Victoria I., N.W. Ter., Can.		
	. . . .	70N	110W
15	Vidin, Bul.	44N	23 E
54	Viedma, Arg.	41S	63W
13	Vienna (Wien), Aus. . . .	48N	16 E
24	Vietnam (Ctry.) Asia . . .	18N	108 E
14	Vigo, Sp.	42N	9W
23	Vijayawāda, India	17N	81 E
27	Vila, Van.	18S	168 E
52	Villa Bella, Bol.	10S	65W
13	Villach, Aus.	47N	14 E
50	Villahermosa, Mex.	18N	93W
54	Villa María, Arg.	32S	63W
54	Villa Mercedes, Arg. . . .	34S	65W
13	Villeurbanne, Fr.	46N	5 E
12	Vilnius, Lith.	55N	25 E
17	Vilyuysk, Russia	64N	122 E
54	Viña del Mar, Chile	33S	72W
12	Vindeln, Swe.	64N	20 E
37	Vineland, N.J.	39N	75W
11	Vinnytsya, Ukr.	49N	29 E
32	Virden, Man., Can.. . . .	50N	101W
36	Virginia, Minn.	48N	93W
35	Virginia (State) U.S. . . .	37N	81W
37	Virginia Beach, Va.	37N	76W
51	Virgin Is., N.A.	18N	63W
23	Vishākhapatnam, India . .	18N	84 E
10	Vitebsk, Bela.	55N	30 E
13	Viterbo, It.	42N	12 E
17	Vitim, Russia	59N	113 E
53	Vitória, Braz.	20S	40W
14	Vitoria, Sp.	43N	3W
22	Vladikavkaz, Russia	43N	45 E
11	Vladimir, Russia	56N	40 E
17	Vladivostok, Russia	43N	132 E
15	Vlorě (Valona), Alb. . . .	40N	20 E
11	Volga (R.) Russia	46N	48 E
11	Volgograd (Stalingrad),		
	Russia	49N	44 E
11	Vologda, Russia	59N	40 E
15	Volos, Grc.	39N	23 E
11	Vol'sk, Russia	52N	47 E
11	Vorkuta, Russia	67N	64 E
11	Voronezh, Russia	52N	39 E
11	Votkinsk, Russia	57N	54 E
15	Voznesens'k, Ukr.	48N	31 E
15	Vratsa, Bul.	43N	24 E
15	Vršac, Yugo.	45N	21 E
10	Vyborg, Russia	61N	29 E
11	Vylkove, Ukr.	45N	30 E
16	Vytegra, Russia	61N	36 E

W

36	Wabash (R.) U.S.	38N	88W
47	Waco, Tex.	32N	97W
24	Waingapu, Indon.	10S	120 E
32	Wainwright, Alta., Can. . .	53N	111W
21	Wakayama, Japan	34N	135 E
21	Wakkanai, Japan	45N	142 E
30	Waku Kundo, Ang.	11S	15 E
13	Wales (Polit. Reg.), U.K.	52N	4W
40	Walla Walla, Wash.	46N	118W
30	Walvis Bay, S. Afr.	23S	14 E
39	Walworth, Wis.	43N	89W
20	Wanxian, China	31N	108 E
23	Warangal, India	18N	80 E
28	Wargla, Alg.	32N	5 E
36	Warren, Mich.	43N	83W
36	Warren, Ohio	41N	81W
37	Warren, Pa.	42N	79W
13	Warsaw (Warszawa), Pol.	52N	21 E
37	Warwick, R.I.	42N	71W
37	Washington, D.C.	39N	77W
37	Washington, Pa.	40N	80W
40	Washington (State) U.S.	47N	121W
37	Waterbury, Conn.	41N	73W
39	Waterloo, Iowa	42N	92W
37	Watertown, N.Y.	44N	76W
38	Watertown, S. Dak.	45N	97W
32	Watrous, Sask., Can. . . .	52N	106W
32	Watson Lake, Yukon, Can.		
	. . . .	60N	129W
36	Waukegan, Ill.	42N	88W
39	Waukesha, Wis.	4N	88W
39	Wausau, Wis.	45N	90W
39	Wauwatosa, Wis.	43N	88W
49	Waycross, Ga.	31N	82W
21	Weifang, China	37N	119 E
13	Weimar, Ger.	51N	11 E
36	Weirton, W. Va.	40N	81W
9	Wellington, N.Z.	41S	175 E
13	Wels, Aus.	48N	14 E
20	Wensu, China	42N	80 E
21	Wenzhou, China	28N	121 E
39	West Allis, Wis.	43N	88W
23	Western Ghāts (Mts.) India		
	. . . .	16N	74 E
28	Western Sahara (Ctry.) Afr.		
	. . . .	25N	14W
8	Western Samoa (Ctry.),		
	Pac. O.	15S	177W
37	West Hartford, Conn. . . .	42N	73W
51	West Indies (Is.) N.A. . . .	18N	73W
36	West Lafayette, Ind.	40N	87W
49	West Palm Beach, Fla. . .	27N	80W
35	West Virginia (State) U.S.	39N	81W
25	Wewak, Pap. N. Gui. . . .	4S	143 E
13	Wexford, Ire.	52N	6W
37	Weymouth, Mass.	43N	71W
37	Wheaton, Md.	39N	77W
36	Wheeling, W. Va.	40N	81W
32	Whitecourt, Alta., Can. . .	54N	116W
32	Whitehorse, Yukon, Can.	61N	135W
42	Whitney, Mt., Calif.	36N	118W
45	Wichita, Kans.	38N	97W
44	Wichita Falls, Tex.	34N	98W
13	Wiener-Neustadt, Aus. . .	48N	16 E
13	Wiesbaden, Ger.	50N	8 E
13	Wilhelmshaven, Ger. . . .	53N	8 E
37	Wilkes-Barre, Pa.	41N	76W
51	Willemstad, Neth. Ant. . .	12N	69W
37	Williamsport, Pa.	41N	77W
38	Williston, N. Dak.	48N	104W
36	Wilmette, Ill.	42N	88W
37	Wilmington, Del.	40N	76W
49	Wilmington, N.C.	34N	78W
30	Windhoek, Nam.	22S	17 E
33	Windsor, Newf., Can. . . .	49N	56W
33	Windsor, Ont., Can. . . .	42N	83W
40	Winnemucca, Nev.	41N	118W
36	Winnetka, Ill.	42N	88W
32	Winnipeg, Man., Can. . .	50N	97W
32	Winnipeg, L., Man., Can.	53N	98W
36	Winona, Minn.	44N	92W
49	Winston-Salem, N.C. . . .	36N	80W
39	Wisconsin (R.) Wis.	43N	90W
39	Wisconsin (State) U.S. . .	44N	91W
39	Wisconsin Dells, Wis. . . .	44N	90W
13	Wisla (Vistula) (R.) Pol. .	53N	19 E
13	Wismar, Ger.	54N	11 E
13	Włocławek, Pol.	52N	19 E
27	Wollongong, Austl.	34S	151 E
13	Wolverhampton, Eng. . . .	53N	2W
21	Wōnsan, Kor.	39N	127 E
39	Woods, Lake of the, Can.-		
	U.S.	49N	95W
37	Woonsocket, R.I.	42N	71W
13	Worcester, Eng.	52N	2W
37	Worcester, Mass.	42N	72W
13	Worms, Ger.	50N	8 E
13	Wrocław (Breslau), Pol. . .	51N	17 E
21	Wuchang, China	31N	114 E
21	Wuhan, China	30N	114 E
13	Wuppertal, Ger.	51N	7 E
21	Wushi, China	41N	79 E
21	Wuxi, China	32N	120 E
21	Wuxing, China	31N	120 E
21	Wuzhou, China	24N	111 E
36	Wyandotte, Mich.	42N	83W
34	Wyoming (State) U.S. . . .	43N	108W

X

15	Xanthi, Grc.	41N	25 E
21	Xiamen, China	24N	118 E
21	Xi'an, China	34N	109 E
21	Xiang (R.) China	26N	113 E
21	Xiangtan, China	28N	113 E
53	Xingu (R.) Braz.	7S	53W
21	Xinhui, China	23N	113 E
20	Xining, China	37N	102 E
21	Xinyang, China	32N	114 E
31	Xuddur, Som.	4N	44 E
21	Xuzhou, China	34N	117 E

Y

40	Yakima, Wash.	47N	120W
17	Yakutsk, Russia	62N	130 E
11	Yalta, Ukr.	44N	34 E
21	Yalu (R.) China-Kor. . . .	41N	126 E
21	Yamagata, Japan	38N	140 E
15	Yambol, Bul.	42N	27 E
28	Yamoussoukro, C. Iv. . . .	7N	4W
17	Yamsk, Russia	60N	154 E
22	Yanbu, Sau. Ar.	24N	38 E
21	Yangtze (Chang) (R.) China		
	. . . .	30N	117 E
38	Yankton, S. Dak.	43N	97W
21	Yantai, China	38N	121 E
31	Yaoundé, Cam.	4N	12 E
16	Yaransk, Russia	57N	48 E
11	Yaroslavl', Russia	58N	40 E
23	Yatung, China	27N	89 E
22	Yazd, Iran	32N	54 E
24	Ye, Mya.	15N	98 E
21	Yecheng, China	37N	79 E
11	Yekaterinburg (Sverdlovsk),		
	Russia	57N	61 E
11	Yelets, Russia	53N	38 E
32	Yellowknife, N.W. Ter.,		
	Can.	62N	115W
21	Yellow Sea, China-Kor. . .	37N	123 E
41	Yellowstone (R.) U.S. . . .	46N	106W
22	Yemen (Ctry.) Asia	15N	47 E
16	Yenisey (R.) Russia	72N	83 E
17	Yeniseysk, Russia	58N	92 E
11	Yerevan, Arm.	40N	44 E
11	Yevpatoriya, Ukr.	45N	33 E
15	Yeysk, Russia	47N	38 E
20	Yibin, China	29N	105 E
21	Yichang, China	31N	111 E
20	Yinchuan, China	38N	106 E
21	Yingkou, China	41N	123 E
20	Yining (Gulja), China . . .	44N	81 E
24	Yogyakarta, Indon.	8S	110 E
21	Yokohama, Japan	36N	140 E
37	Yonkers, N.Y.	41N	74W
13	York, Eng.	54N	1W
37	York, Pa.	40N	77W
32	Yorkton, Sask., Can. . . .	51N	103W
21	Yoshkar-Ola, Russia	57N	48 E
36	Youngstown, Ohio	41N	81W
22	Yrghyz, Kaz.	48N	61 E
15	Yugoslavia (Ctry.) Eur. . .	45N	17 E
34	Yukon (R.) Can.-U.S. . . .	63N	160W
32	Yukon (Ter.) Can.	63N	135W
43	Yuma, Ariz.	33N	115W
20	Yumen, China	40N	97 E
20	Yutian (Keriya), China . . .	37N	82 E

Z

13	Zabrze, Pol.	50N	19 E
50	Zacatecas, Mex.	23N	103W
14	Zadar, Cro.	44N	15 E
15	Zagreb, Cro.	46N	16 E
22	Zagros Mts., Iran	34N	48 E
22	Zāhedān, Iran	30N	61 E
13	Zahlah, Leb.	34N	36 E
30	Zaire (Ctry.) Afr.	1S	23 E
31	Zambezi (R.) Afr.	16S	30 E
30	Zambia (Ctry.) Afr.	15S	28 E
25	Zamboanga, Phil.	7N	122 E
14	Zamora, Sp.	42N	6W
13	Zamość, Pol.	51N	23 E
36	Zanesville, Ohio	40N	82W
22	Zanjān, Iran	36N	48 E
31	Zanzibar (I.) Tan.	6S	39 E
10	Zapadnaya Dvina (R.) Eur.		
	. . . .	57N	24 E
11	Zaporizhzhya		
	(Zaporozh'ye), Ukr. . . .	48N	35 E
14	Zaragoza, Sp.	42N	1W
54	Zarate, Arg.	34S	59W
17	Zashiversk, Russia	67N	143 E
21	Zavitinsk, Russia	50N	130 E
16	Zemlya Frantsa Iosifa (Is.)		
	Russia	80N	50 E
15	Zemun, Yugo.	45N	20 E
17	Zeya, Russia	54N	127 E
16	Zhambyl, Kaz.	43N	71 E
22	Zhangaqazaly, Kaz.	46N	62 E
21	Zhangjiakou, China	41N	115 E
21	Zhangzhou, China	25N	118 E
21	Zhanjiang, China	21N	110 E
21	Zhengzhou, China	35N	114 E
21	Zhenjiang, China	32N	119 E
17	Zhigansk, Russia	67N	123 E
10	Zhytomyr, Ukr.	50N	29 E
13	Žilina, Slov.	49N	19 E
30	Zimbabwe (Ctry.) Afr. . .	19S	30 E
30	Zomba, Malawi	15S	35 E
15	Zonguldak, Tur.	41N	32 E
20	Zunyi, China	28N	107 E
13	Zürich, Switz.	47N	9 E
15	Zvenyhorodka, Ukr.	49N	31 E
13	Zwickau, Ger.	51N	12 E
13	Zwolle, Neth.	53N	6 E
16	Zyryan, Kaz.	50N	84 E